TRUST + FOLLOW

TRUST +

FOLLOW

A 60-DAY DEVOTIONAL TO KNOW JESUS MORE

MADDIE JOY FISCHER

BakerBooks

a division of Baker Publishing Group

BakerBooks.com

© 2024 by Maddie Joy Fischer

Published by Baker Books
a division of Baker Publishing Group
Grand Rapids, Michigan
BakerBooks.com

Printed in China

Library of Congress Cataloging-in-Publication Data
Names: Fischer, Maddie Joy, author.
Title: Trust + follow : a 60-day devotional to know Jesus more / Maddie Joy Fischer.
Other titles: Trust and follow
Description: Grand Rapids, Michigan : Baker Books, a division of Baker Publishing
    Group, [2024]
Identifiers: LCCN 2023043293 | ISBN 9781540904003 (cloth) | ISBN 9781493445783
    (ebook)
Subjects: LCSH: Young women—Prayers and devotions. | Young women—Religious
    life. | Devotional calendars.
Classification: LCC BV4860 .F59 2024 | DDC 242/.63—dc23/eng/20240220
LC record available at https://lccn.loc.gov/2023043293

Interior design by William Overbeeke

Cover design by Laura Powell
Cover illustration © Orkney by Dan Hobday

Published in association with Books & Such Literary Management, www.booksand
such.com.

Baker Publishing Group publications use paper produced from sustainable forestry
practices and postconsumer waste whenever possible.

24 25 26 27 28 29 30   7 6 5 4 3 2 1

To my parents (and pastors),
BRIAN and JOY KITCHEN,
for teaching me what it looks like
to know and follow Jesus
and to take Him at His word.
I wouldn't be writing this devotional
if it wasn't for your belief in Him
and your belief in me.
I love and honor you
wholeheartedly.

—Firstborn

CONTENTS

Introduction   8

INTRODUCTION

If you are reading these words, it's not by coincidence. I trust that God is intentional and perfect in all of His ways. I write these words with tear-filled eyes and in complete awe of His goodness. I wish I could catch you up to the point in my story where writing this devotional came to be. Maybe someday I will, but for now I'll sum it up by saying that one step of obedience after another has led me to this moment.

More often than not, I haven't known where I was going, but with every surrendered step, I have grown in confidence that the One I am following surely will not lead me astray. Jesus never has and He never will. The more I follow Him, the more my trust in His goodness increases. I move forward continually in the decision that I will follow Him wherever He leads, no matter the cost. It is costly, but I can assure you that the reward is far greater than what it requires. His way has rarely led me to the expected road, but He has been faithful with every step.

I can't tell you how your story will unfold, but I can assure you that the best things in this life will come as a result of knowing, trusting, and following Jesus—not the easiest things, but the best, most abundant things. Proverbs 3:5–6 has become such a thematic passage in my life, selected out of the realization that only in complete surrender have I experienced the abundance of knowing and walking with Jesus. I desire for everyone to experience that abundance. I can't live it out for you, but I can share my experiences, point you in His direction, and encourage you to wholeheartedly follow Him. That's my heart behind this devotional: to provide you with a resource to grow in understanding who Jesus is, what His Word says, and what that means for you personally.

Wherever you find yourself in this journey of taking Him at His word, as you read these pages, I pray that you will grow in knowledge of the truth, boldness to live out and proclaim it, and love for the One who it's all about—Jesus! I pray that as you prioritize dwelling in His presence daily, you will experience the evidence of His goodness undeniably and that He will increase your desire to live a life that points people in His direction.

There is nothing better than a relationship with your Creator, Savior, Father, and closest friend; it's what you were created for. His Word applied, delivers. It never returns void.

He will be found faithful to His word and true to His character in the lives of those who know Him and follow His lead. His plans for you are good, and they will prevail.

Over the next sixty days, I invite you along this journey of knowing Jesus more than you did before. I challenge you to be sincere in seeking, honest in reflection, and expectant for His truth to begin or continue to transform your heart and your life as you apply it.

I know firsthand that if you give Him your wholehearted yes, He will do more with it for His glory than you could have ever imagined.

MADDIE JOY

KNOW, TRUST, AND FOLLOW

Trust in the LORD with all your heart
    and lean not on your own understanding;
in all your ways submit to him,
    and he will make your paths straight.

Proverbs 3:5–6

There is nothing better than knowing, trusting, and following Jesus. You will find Him faithful to His character and true to His word in your life as you follow His lead.

LET ME INVITE YOU into the process of titling this devotional because it was very intentional. Generally speaking, you can't trust someone you don't know, and you won't follow someone you don't trust. Therefore, this journey has to begin and end with knowing Jesus. It's one thing to know of someone, but it's another to know them personally. There is a huge difference between acquaintanceship and relationship.

Too many people—yes, even people who are raised in the church—spend their lives knowing of Jesus but are still outside of a personal relationship with Him. I can only imagine how it breaks His heart. Jesus doesn't want to be your acquaintance; He wants to be your closest friend. He desires a relationship with His children, but as long as any one of us lives outside of a relationship with Him, we are missing out on what we are made for.

Without knowing Him personally, you can't graduate to the adventure of trusting and following Him. If you don't know Jesus personally, know that He is inviting you to make the best decision you've ever made—getting to know Him. If you do know Him, know that He wants to grow deeper in relationship with you daily, equip you to introduce others to Him, and lead you further along the path of His perfect plan for your life. He will be faithful to complete what He has started in you.

The more you know Jesus, the more your life will be transformed by the truth of His Word. It's a never-ending process on this side of heaven. A life of surrender is a life lived in response to the knowledge of who God is and trust in what He says. The evidence of us truly knowing Him is our willingness to do what

> A life of surrender is a life lived in response to the knowledge of who God is and trust in what He says.

He instructs. Everything He instructs is intentional and purposeful. Are you living a life that reflects your trust in that promise?

Continually exchange your own plan and preference for whatever He has in mind. Your own plan will fail you, but He never will. God's ways are higher than your mind can comprehend. You may not always know or understand what He is doing, but if you know, trust, and follow Him, He will continually leave you in awe of His goodness. Ask yourself this question today, If my obedience to God's Word is the evidence of my love for Him, am I living like I love Him?

> We know that we have come to know him if we keep his commands.
>
> **1 John 2:3**

PRAYER: Jesus, grow me in the knowledge of who You are and the application of Your Word to my life. Thank You that as I follow You, You lead me step by step. Amen.

REFLECTION/APPLICATION: What have you put before your desire to know Jesus more? How do you want to grow in knowing, trusting, and following Him in the days to come?

ABIDE + REMAIN

Remain in me, as I also remain in you. No branch can bear
fruit by itself; it must remain in the vine. Neither can you
bear fruit unless you remain in me.

John 15:4

> You are called, first and foremost, to continually grow
> in relationship with Jesus. As you remain in Him, the rest
> will follow.

WHOLEHEARTEDLY BELIEVE that the Lord wants to do
unimaginable things with unlikely people who take Him at
His word.

Here's the thing though, doing "big things" for God but not
walking closely in relationship with Him is not a life we should
be interested in living. We are called, first and foremost, to a
relationship with Jesus. Everything else should follow.

Our human nature causes us to quickly fall into patterns of
striving, performance, and even craving the glory that is His

> Our ability has nothing to do with who we are and everything to do with the source we connect our lives to.

alone. These patterns disconnect us from the One we proclaim to live for. It's heartbreaking but true that so many people are doing things for Jesus while living disconnected from Him. This was never His plan. Many say it's all about Him, but the posture of their hearts tells a different story at times. I've been there, and it's an empty place to be.

When we desire to be used by God more than we desire to fellowship with Him daily, we find ourselves in a dangerous and distant place, outside of His desire for us.

Our ability has nothing to do with who we are and everything to do with the source we connect our lives to. Jesus provides us with a picture of Him as the vine and us as the branches to remind us that we can do nothing worthwhile apart from Him. True success in life will always be a result of connectedness to Him. When we disconnect from the source, we cut ourselves off from the nourishment of spiritual life.

The best advice I can give to anyone who has a sincere heart to be used by God is to spend time with Him daily. Don't just talk to or ask things of Him; take time to listen to His voice. Pursue Him before anything or anyone else. The dreams, desires, and gifts you have been given were intentionally given to you to advance His kingdom on earth. Thank Him for that. Ask Jesus to make you more like Him every day and to use you in whatever ways will most bring Him glory. When He answers, be sure to give Him ALL the glory.

Remember, you can do nothing worthwhile apart from Him. The fruit of your life will always be a natural result of remaining connected to Him. Stay near to His heart, treasure His Word, and take Him at His word. Love what you get to do for Him, but always love Him more!

> Blessed is the one
>   who does not walk in step with the wicked
> or stand in the way that sinners take
>   or sit in the company of mockers,
> but whose delight is in the law of the Lord,
>   and who meditates on his law day and night.
> That person is like a tree planted by streams of water,
>   which yields its fruit in season
> and whose leaf does not wither—
>   whatever they do prospers.
>
> **Psalm 1:1–3**

PRAYER: Jesus, help me to live in pursuit of You first. Use the dreams, desires, and gifts You have given me for Your glory. Amen.

REFLECTION/APPLICATION: What does this picture of Jesus as the vine and you as the branch tell you about your need for Him? Why is it important that you desire to know Him and love Him more than you desire to be used by Him?

A SOUND MIND

For God has not given us a spirit of fear, but of power and of love and of a sound mind.

2 Timothy 1:7 NKJV

> The promise of a sound mind isn't dependent on your circumstances but on your trust in the One who is sovereign over them. Settle your heart and mind in God's promises and you will live in His peace.

I WILL NEVER HAVE a sound mind as long as I believe it will arrive in the package of a more ideal set of circumstances. A sound mind is a direct result of a heart settled on the promises of God.

It's important to be honest with ourselves and, more importantly, the Lord. We need to ask Him to identify the areas in our lives where we aren't taking Him at His word as much as we would like to say that we are. To take Him at His word doesn't mean we can't make our requests known and have hopes, dreams, desires for a certain outcome, or even have a clear answer. Trusting Him ultimately requires us to hold our own plans with a loose grip and yield to His way.

Although the answers aren't as clear as Him physically sitting with us, He has given us His Word and sent His Spirit to guide us. That's where faith really comes in. The best way to grow in faith is to live it. God is still speaking today, but we have to be willing to step back from the busyness of our routines long enough to listen to His voice.

Find rest today in simply doing what is instructed of you and believing that's enough—to know God's Word, to love it, and to live by it.

Every word of the Bible is written with you and me in mind. Rest in the reality that change may not look like a different set of circumstances in the timing you hoped, but it will come through a transformed heart in the waiting, the unknown, and the in-between. Your circumstances will never change God's goodness; He is always good. That's one of the most vital things we will ever learn.

On this day-by-day journey, I am releasing the grip of what has stood in the way of the soundness of heart and mind that comes with a posture of wholehearted trust, and I invite you to do the same. It's a journey. It really is. It's a journey that overflows with

A sound mind is a direct result
of a heart settled
on the promises of God.

grace, and thank Jesus for that, because I don't know about you, but I need every ounce of it.

> And the peace of God, which surpasses all understanding, will guard your hearts and your minds in Christ Jesus.
>
> **Philippians 4:7 ESV**

PRAYER: Jesus, I pray for a sound mind that stems from a heart settled on Your promises. Thank You for Your grace in the journey. Amen.

REFLECTION/APPLICATION: Write down a list of some things you are currently fearful of or anxious about. Then, write about how the Scriptures in today's devotion help combat those fears.

YOU ARE (SO) LOVED

For God so loved the world, that he gave his only Son, that whoever believes in him should not perish but have eternal life.

John 3:16 ESV

This is the gospel, the sacrifice of love that made a way for our salvation. Live in awareness that you are loved with an unconditional and everlasting love.

I WAS LEADING WORSHIP for the youth group at my church one Sunday evening, and as we sang about the love of Jesus, He whispered these words to my heart, "The most important thing you will ever know is My love for you." It moved me into overwhelming gratitude but also sorrow and repentance about how quickly I forget the way His love changed everything for me and the fact that He is all that I need.

At that moment, I felt led to address each student in the room by their name followed by these three words—"Jesus loves you." As I yielded to His interruption and began to speak the love of Jesus over the students in the room, an altar full of tear-stained eyes looked back at me. Despite our many differences, what unified every one of us in the room was our desperate need for the only thing that satisfies—the unconditional, transforming love of Jesus. That same thing unifies you and me.

Psalm 63:3 reminds us of the incomparable value of His love.

> Your unfailing love is better than life itself;
>   how I praise you! (NLT)

There is a lot of truth to unpack in the days ahead, but you need to know that it all starts and ends with this simple truth: whoever you are, whatever you are doing, wherever you find yourself in this very moment, and no matter how many times you have heard it: [Insert your name here], Jesus loves you.

We would be lost without His love. The love of Jesus restored our relationship with Him because sin once separated us from the ability to walk with Him. We can't strive enough to earn it, and we will never be able to do enough to deserve it. Everything He does is because of His love for us. Everything He instructs us in is for our good.

[Insert your name here],
Jesus loves you.

His love is unconditional and unchanging. He knows every-thing about us yet loves us all the same. In order to live out this abundant life, we simply must receive His love and live like we believe we are loved.

> And I pray that you, being rooted and established in love, may have power, together with all the Lord's holy people, to grasp how wide and long and high and deep is the love of Christ, and to know this love that surpasses knowledge— that you may be filled to the measure of all the fullness of God.
>
> **Ephesians 3:17–19**

PRAYER: Jesus, help me to live like I am abundantly and unconditionally loved by You, because I am. Thank You for Your sacrifice that restored my ability to walk in rela-tionship with You. Amen.

REFLECTION/APPLICATION: What have you tried to find satisfaction in other than the love of Jesus? If someone asked you how Jesus's unconditional love has changed your life, how would you respond?

DAY 5

KEEP HIS COMMANDS

If you love me, keep my commands.

John 14:15

God's love and grace aren't excuses to continue living in sinful patterns. Your love for Jesus should lead to the desire not only to know His Word but also to live out what it says.

THE BIBLE ISN'T just a book of stories and suggestions; it is the living, breathing Word of God that needs to be activated in and applied to our lives. As you surrender your life to the One whose plans for you are good and who wants to give you hope and a future, you will experience the fullness that comes only as a result of knowing and following Him. You will live in these promises:

His joy

His hope

His peace

His provision

His protection

His blessing

His strength

The list goes on and on.

God's Word proves itself reliable and true in the lives of those who love Him and walk according to His Word. As it is tested through the mountains and valleys of our days and generations, His Word will remain unchanging and unfailing. You may not always know where you are going, but He does, and He knows how to get you there. He is intentional in all that He does and kind in every step He orchestrates.

You will see the evidence that when you pray, God hears, and when you call upon His name, He answers. You will learn (maybe

> God's Word proves itself reliable and true in the lives of those who love Him and walk according to His Word.

the hard way) that the answer may not always come at the moment or in the package you hoped for. But it will always be right on time and better than expected because He does exceedingly and abundantly more than what we could ask or imagine. He is working all things out for our good and His glory.

No matter where we find ourselves in this journey with Jesus, I want to challenge each one of us to ask ourselves this question, Does the life I am living reflect my confidence that God's Word is true?

God's intention for the lives of those who He loves and who love Him is better than we could ever dream, but we won't experience this reality without continually applying His truth to our lives. He is who He says He is, and He does what He says He will do.

Trust Him.

> Do not merely listen to the word, and so deceive yourselves. Do what it says. Anyone who listens to the word but does not do what it says is like someone who looks at his face in a mirror and, after looking at himself, goes away and immediately forgets what he looks like. But whoever looks intently into the perfect law that gives freedom, and continues in it—not forgetting what they have heard, but doing it—they will be blessed in what they do.
>
> **James 1:22–25**

PRAYER: Jesus, help me to know and apply Your Word in every area of my life. Create in me a desire to surrender patterns and habits in my life that don't align with Your Word. Amen.

REFLECTION/APPLICATION: Why is it important not only to know but also to apply God's Word to your life? How does your life currently reflect your confidence that God's Word is true? How could it better reflect this confidence?

FIRM FOUNDATION

Therefore everyone who hears these words of mine and puts them into practice is like a wise man who built his house on the rock. The rain came down, the streams rose, and the winds blew and beat against that house; yet it did not fall, because it had its foundation on the rock. But everyone who hears these words of mine and does not put them into practice is like a foolish man who built his house on sand. The rain came down, the streams rose, and the winds blew and beat against that house, and it fell with a great crash.

Matthew 7:24–27

Trials and change will reveal whether your life is built on the Rock or sinking sand. Build your life on Jesus, and you won't be moved.

MY DAD ONCE SAID, "You can cut corners with a countertop, not when laying a foundation."

The two houses talked about in this passage from Matthew 7 may look very similar. The one built on the sand may even appear better or more desirable from the outside looking in. It might be bigger and there could be more expensive cars parked in the driveway, but when the storm comes, the way the home looks isn't what's important. When the storm comes, the house built on the sand is coming down, and the house built on the Rock will remain standing.

I fear that culturally we have become so consumed with what our lives look like that we have forgotten that what is most important is the foundation on which we are building them. I find it interesting that the most important part is the part that's unseen.

I get it. It's nice to have nice things. Finances, followers, cars, and aesthetics all seem really important, but the reality is, all of these things are fleeting. They have no eternal value. I'm not saying there is anything wrong with having nice things. But I am saying we can't build our life and our hope upon them.

The question we need to ask ourselves is, What will stand when the storm comes?

There are two very important things you need to know: (1) storms will come, and (2) Jesus is the only foundation that will not move.

Storms in life will come. Live prepared to face this inevitable reality. At one time or another, and most likely many times, you will face trials, tribulation, tragedy, hardship, and devastation. Sometimes you will expect it and have time to prepare and sometimes you won't. Life will bring the wind, the rain, and the waves, and at times, it will knock the wind right out of you.

You can't control everything you experience, but you do get to choose the foundation on which you build your life.

You can't control everything
you experience, but you do get
to choose the foundation on
which you build your life.

As many around us build their lives on sinking sand, may we be the ones who build our lives on the Rock of Jesus. He will never be shaken.

Jesus Christ is the same yesterday and today and forever.
Hebrews 13:8

PRAYER: Jesus, help me to build my life on You so I remain immovable in the midst of the storms I face in life. Thank You that You are constant no matter what changes around me. Amen.

REFLECTION/APPLICATION: What are some examples of "sinking sand" that you are tempted to build your life on? What can be learned from the storms you face in life?

DAY 7

SEEK HIM + SEE HIM

You will seek me and find me when you seek me with all
your heart.

Jeremiah 29:13

God promises that those who seek Him will find
Him. Seek Him in everything and you will see Him in
everything.

ONE OF MY FAVORITE characteristics of God is His trustworthiness. He doesn't make a promise He can't or doesn't
intend to keep. Every word He speaks is true, and He will fulfill it.
That is the evidence of His faithfulness. Some of those promises,
though, require something of us. A great example of this is found
in Jeremiah 29:13. Take a moment to read it again: "You will seek
me and find me when you seek me with all your heart."

The requirement is to seek Him, and the promise is that He
will be found. When I think about this, I'm reminded of playing
hide-and-seek with my parents when I was a little girl. When

> As we continue to seek Him throughout our lives, He continues to reveal Himself to us.

it was my turn to seek, they would hide in a place where they could easily be found. They weren't trying to trick me. I still had to look for them, but they hid in places that made my job easy. They *wanted* me to find them.

It's the same with you and God. He is not playing a game of hide-and-seek with us or trying to trip us up. He's not hiding in impossible-to-find places, hoping we will give up and quit looking. No, He wants us to find Him, but He also wants us to intentionally seek Him. The seeking develops our desire. It reminds us of our desperate need for Jesus, and it deepens our longing for more of Him.

Finding Jesus is only the beginning; He longs for us to continually grow in relationship with Him. He has so much more for us. As we continue to seek Him throughout our lives, He continues to reveal Himself to us. That's the beauty of a relationship.

I remember my mom once praying, "Jesus, help us to see You in everything because we seek You in everything."

I echo that prayer over you today. I pray that you see Jesus in everything because you choose to seek Him in everything—daily, diligently, and with desperation.

When you seek Him, you will find Him. Your loving Father is never far from you.

> So I say to you: Ask and it will be given to you; seek and
> you will find; knock and the door will be opened to you. For
> everyone who asks receives; the one who seeks finds; and
> to the one who knocks, the door will be opened.
>
> **Luke 11:9–10**

PRAYER: Jesus, help me to see You in everything because I seek You in everything. Thank You for the promise that when I seek You, I will find You. Amen.

REFLECTION/APPLICATION: What is one of your favorite characteristics of God? Why is it important that your pursuit of Jesus is CONTINUAL? How do you see the evidence of who He is in this current moment?

DAY 8

HIGHS + LOWS

"Though the mountains be shaken
   and the hills be removed,
yet my unfailing love for you will not be shaken
   nor my covenant of peace be removed,"
   says the LORD, who has compassion on you.

Isaiah 54:10

The God of the mountains is the God of the valleys. In order to believe that, you will have to experience His faithfulness in both places.

NO MATTER WHAT you have faced in the past, God was still God.

No matter what you are faced with today, God is still God.

No matter what you will face tomorrow, God will still be God.

Saying that the God of the mountains is the God of the valleys isn't just a catchy phrase; it is the hope that we have to carry us

> ## God's faithfulness doesn't change when you find yourself in the valley.

through life, that the promise of who He is, is unchanging and unfailing everywhere we go.

He is the God of the mountains and the God of the valleys.

He is the God of the highs and the God of the lows.

He is also the God of everything in-between, and you will spend the majority of your life in the in-between. You must learn to trust Him there.

He goes before you, He is behind you, and He surrounds you on every side. He is always with you and always for you. It's easy to recognize Him on the mountaintop, but we're quick to forget His goodness in the valley.

God's faithfulness doesn't change when you find yourself in the valley. He is in it all. Throughout my journey I have learned that it's often in the valley where God has most revealed Himself to me. It's often in the valley that I've most seen His glory on display. If I never walked through it, there would be so many things about who God is that I wouldn't have personally experienced and, as a result with so many things I wouldn't be able to share about His goodness to the world around me.

In darkness, I've seen Him as the Light.

In sorrow, I've seen Him as my joy.

In lack, I've seen His hand of provision.

In loneliness, I've seen Him as my unfailing friend.

In heartbreak and sickness, I've seen Him as the Healer and
    Promise Keeper.

In anxiety, I've seen Him as my peace.

In fear, I've seen Him as my comfort and my protector.

In the unknown, I've seen Him as the one thing I can remain
    certain of.

In change, I've seen Him as my constant.

In disappointment, I've seen Him as the lifter of my head.

You should celebrate Him on the mountaintop, but the true
test of faith is your ability to trust Him and celebrate His goodness
in the low of the valley and in the unknown of the in-between.

He is God, and He is good, even in the valley.

> Where can I go from your Spirit?
>   Where can I flee from your presence?
> If I go up to the heavens, you are there;
>   if I make my bed in the depths, you are there.
> If I rise on the wings of the dawn,
>   if I settle on the far side of the sea,
> even there your hand will guide me,
>   your right hand will hold me fast.
>   **Psalm 139:7–10**

PRAYER: Jesus, help me to trust You through the hard-
ships and valley seasons of my life. Thank You that You
are with me through every high and low. Amen.

REFLECTION/APPLICATION: What has God taught
you through both a high (mountaintop) and low (valley) moment in your life? How would you describe the
current season you are in, and what is He teaching you
through it?

SET APART

But you are not like that, for you are a chosen people. You
are royal priests, a holy nation, God's very own possession.
As a result, you can show others the goodness of God, for
he called you out of the darkness into his wonderful light.

1 Peter 2:9 NLT

God calls His people out of darkness and into the light.
Live in the light and as a result His goodness will be
revealed in and through you.

TO SET SOMETHING APART means to separate it and
keep it for a special purpose. You are called, chosen, and set
apart for the special purpose of heaven invading earth. Your life
should be evidence to everyone you encounter of the goodness
and glory of God. It's not always an easy task, but it is an honor.
It's costly more than it's convenient, but the reward is far greater
than the cost. It is worth everything it requires.

The lives of those who are set apart should look clearly different from the lives of those around them. This instruction is given in 1 John 2:15–17:

> Do not love the world or anything in the world. If anyone loves the world, love for the Father is not in them. For everything in the world—the lust of the flesh, the lust of the eyes, and the pride of life—comes not from the Father but from the world. The world and its desires pass away, but whoever does the will of God lives forever.

We are called to be holy as He is holy, not in our own strength but through His strength and power at work within us. Knowing His Word is one thing, but living it is another. God's Word, when applied, will continually transform us to be more like Him. It's through being like Him that the world around us will see Him in and through us.

You have been called out of darkness and into the light, so live in the light! Don't hide your light or run back to the darkness. You have a story of redemption to tell that others need to hear, and it can be told through the way you live, not just what you say. Answer the call of living set apart daily so that people will come to know who Jesus is through your actions and your

> Knowing His Word is one thing,
> but living it is another.

deeds. Tell of His love that changed everything. Let His Word be the standard you live according to.

Be who He has called you to be and do what He has called you to do. Living for the purpose of furthering the name of Jesus is the greatest purpose you can live for. It's a joy to be set apart for His name's sake.

> For the grace of God has appeared that offers salvation to all people. It teaches us to say "No" to ungodliness and worldly passions, and to live self-controlled, upright and godly lives in this present age, while we wait for the blessed hope—the appearing of the glory of our great God and Savior, Jesus Christ, who gave himself for us to redeem us from all wickedness and to purify for himself a people that are his very own, eager to do what is good.
>
> **Titus 2:11–14**

PRAYER: Jesus, help me to prioritize what is honoring to You over what is convenient for me. Thank You for equipping me through Your Word to live set apart for Your glory. Amen.

REFLECTION/APPLICATION: What are some differences between desires of the flesh and godly desires? Why is it important that our lives look different from those in the world around us?

KEPT BY GRACE

For it is by grace you have been saved, through faith—and this is not from yourselves, it is the gift of God—not by works, so that no one can boast.

Ephesians 2:8-9

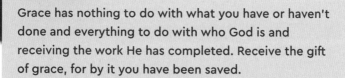

Grace has nothing to do with what you have or haven't done and everything to do with who God is and receiving the work He has completed. Receive the gift of grace, for by it you have been saved.

WE WERE SINGING "Amazing Grace" at church one Sunday. As we sang, I remember a whisper in my heart that said, "Not only are you found but you are kept."

I'll never forget the new understanding of God's goodness and grace I gained in that moment. Many friends in my life had left, so it was hard for me to comprehend that Jesus never would. Maybe you can relate. He wants you to live securely in the promise that you are kept.

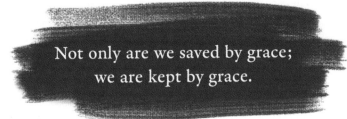

Not only are we saved by grace;
we are kept by grace.

You need to know that grace isn't just some cliché word; it is our lifeline as believers. Our Creator knew that even on our very best day, we couldn't live up to His standard of perfection, so He gave the gift of His amazing, saving grace. Not only are we saved by grace; we are kept by grace. Without it, you and I would be hopeless. The gift of grace is our only hope, and He has given it freely. Just like we can't earn God's love, we can't earn God's grace; we simply have to recognize it has been given to us and receive it. Similar to His love, His grace never runs out.

It's not easy to receive something we feel so undeserving of. Remember today that this gift has nothing to do with who you are but who He is. You are a flawed human who will fall short, but He is a good, faithful, and unfailing Father.

People may have failed you, abandoned you, or forgotten you, but He never will.

He doesn't find us then forsake us.

He doesn't find us then forget us.

He doesn't rescue us only to abandon us when we fail.

He never stops calling us back to Himself.

Grace isn't a give-and-take gift. It's the gift that keeps on giving. It's important that we recognize that grace is not an excuse to live in habitual sin but a covering of love over our imperfections.

I don't know who or where I would be without His gift of grace, and thankfully I don't have to.

Because of grace, you are found, freed, forgiven, and kept. What a promise. What a hope. What a Savior.

> Out of his fullness we have all received grace in place of grace already given.
>
> **John 1:16**

PRAYER: Jesus, help me to walk in the grace You have freely given. Thank You not only that You found me but that You keep me as well. Amen.

REFLECTION/APPLICATION: Have you ever allowed the failure of people to affect your belief in God's faithfulness? What did today's devotion teach or remind you about God's grace and how you should live in response to it?

EVERY DETAIL

The LORD directs the steps of the godly.
He delights in every detail of their lives.
Though they stumble, they will never fall,
for the LORD holds them by the hand.

Psalm 37:23–24 NLT

God's involvement in the details of our lives is far beyond what we will ever be able to comprehend. Since He delights in every detail, we have nothing to fear.

CAME ACROSS this passage from Psalm 37 during a time when I felt like maybe God had forgotten His promises to me. I felt overlooked, lonely, and even like I lacked some of the things I needed. I knew it wasn't true, but I needed to be reminded how much He really cared for me personally and the ways He was intentionally working in my life. He showed up right on time just like He always does.

> He holds the world in His hands
> yet delights in every detail of our lives.

He holds the world in His hands yet delights in every detail of our lives. Take a moment to really think about this; your Creator holds the whole world in His hands, yet He delights in every detail of your life, from the most minuscule to the biggest. He created all things, yet we, His people, are His most prized possession. It's overwhelming and beyond our understanding, but it's who God is. He is sovereign, miraculous, and all-powerful, but He is also relational, intentional, and so loving. Not one or the other but all of the above.

He could have made you anyone or anything, but He made you, YOU.

He could have put you on this earth at any moment in time, but He chose right NOW.

It's no accident, coincidence, or mistake. He is intentional and purposeful in all that He does and designs. Not only does He delight in every detail of your life but He is also ordering your steps and leading you along the path of His perfect plan. When it seems that you are taking the long way or a detour, know that it's better to take the long way with Jesus than the short way without Him.

Rest in the reminder today that there isn't a detail of your life that is unknown to God. You are His treasure. Here are some truths from His Word to prove it.

> Because you are precious in my eyes,
>   and honored, and I love you,
> I give men in return for you,
>   peoples in exchange for your life.
>   **Isaiah 43:4 ESV**

> For you are a people holy to the LORD your God, and the LORD
> has chosen you to be a people for his treasured possession,
> out of all the peoples who are on the face of the earth.
>   **Deuteronomy 14:2 ESV**

> What is the price of two sparrows—one copper coin? But
> not a single sparrow can fall to the ground without your
> Father knowing it. And the very hairs on your head are all
> numbered. So don't be afraid; you are more valuable to God
> than a whole flock of sparrows.
>   **Matthew 10:29–31 NLT**

When you really believe that these things are true, you have nothing to fear. Surrendering your life to Jesus takes the pressure off you to have everything figured out. You are simply called to follow the One who is directing your every step.

PRAYER: Jesus, remind me when I'm worried that You delight in every detail of my life. Thank You that I don't have to fear because You don't miss a thing. Amen.

REFLECTION/APPLICATION: Why is it important not to give our thoughts, feelings, and emotions authority above God's Word? What fears and concerns are eliminated by the promise that He delights in every detail of your life and is ordering your every step?

DAY 12

PROMISE KEEPER

Your kingdom is an everlasting kingdom,
and your dominion endures through all
generations.

The Lord is trustworthy in all he promises
and faithful in all he does.

Psalm 145:13

> People will fail you. God never makes a promise He can't
> keep. He always follows through with His word.

HAVE YOU EVER THOUGHT about the purpose of a pinky
promise? It's an agreement created out of fear that a person's word isn't enough. It's a silly concept with a deep reality.
People are difficult to trust, especially with the things that matter most to us.

Two inevitable realities in your lifetime are that people will
fail you and you will fail people. We will all be disappointed
by people, and we will all disappoint people. When we expect

anyone, even those closest to us, to be for us what only Jesus can be, we will end up heartbroken, let down, disappointed, or all of the above. No matter how hard we try, we will all fall short of perfection. It's something every human has in common, no matter how good we seem or attempt to be.

There is only one perfect person. There is only one person who has never and will never fail, fall short, or go back on His word. Christ is the only One who can carry the weight of the world and the weight of your expectations. Not only will He uphold your expectations, He will far exceed them. You will never have to ask Him to make a pinky promise because His Word is His word.

If you build your life on the Promise Keeper, the foundation won't fail. His character is consistent. His promises are true. He has proven Himself faithful, generation after generation. It's not in His nature to fail, fall short, or lie.

Having good intentions is one thing; following through is another. We often have good intentions, but we are imperfect in our follow-through. Jesus is faithful in His follow-through every time, and He is always right on time—not a moment too early or too late. You may not always understand what He is doing in the moment, but you can trust that His ways are higher. You

> If you build your life
> on the Promise Keeper,
> the foundation won't fail.

may even wish He would do things differently, but His way will always prove better.

Live your life in confident trust in the One who is trustworthy in all that He promises and faithful in all that He does. When all else fails, He won't.

> For no matter how many promises God has made, they are "Yes" in Christ. And so through him the "Amen" is spoken by us to the glory of God.
>
> **2 Corinthians 1:20**

PRAYER: Jesus, help me to find satisfaction in You alone. Increase my confident trust in Your faithfulness as the Promise Keeper. Amen.

REFLECTION/APPLICATION: What lies have become loud in your heart and mind that need to be replaced with the truth of His Word? In what area(s) do you need to trust God to keep His promises?

PRIORITIZE HIS PRESENCE

But seek first his kingdom and his righteousness, and all these things will be given to you as well.

Matthew 6:33

The fruit of your life will reveal your time (or lack of time) spent in God's presence. Prioritize His presence; it will transform your life.

ONE OF THE MOST impactful messages I've ever heard was about the danger of living a life that appears productive but is ultimately disconnected from Jesus. You can appear to be doing all of the right things but miss the main thing. Yes, what you do for God's glory is important, but nothing is more important than your personal relationship with Him. Your greatest calling is not to do things for Him but to dwell in Him.

> You can appear to be doing
> all of the right things
> but miss the main thing.

We see this reality when Jesus gives us a picture of Himself as the vine and us as the branches in John 15:1–8.

> I am the true vine, and my Father is the gardener. He cuts off every branch in me that bears no fruit, while every branch that does bear fruit he prunes so that it will be even more fruitful. You are already clean because of the word I have spoken to you. Remain in me, as I also remain in you. No branch can bear fruit by itself; it must remain in the vine. Neither can you bear fruit unless you remain in me.
>
> I am the vine; you are the branches. If you remain in me and I in you, you will bear much fruit; apart from me you can do nothing. If you do not remain in me, you are like a branch that is thrown away and withers; such branches are picked up, thrown into the fire and burned. If you remain in me and my words remain in you, ask whatever you wish, and it will be done for you. This is to my Father's glory, that you bear much fruit, showing yourselves to be my disciples.

This passage reveals our need for connection to Him as His creation and as His children. We were created for a relationship with Him, and we can't be who He has called us to be and do what He has called us to do without that connection. He didn't have to design us that way, but He did, because He desires to know us and for us to know Him. You become like those you spend the most time with. You can't know someone you don't spend time with.

If I could give you one piece of advice, it would be to prioritize your pursuit of Jesus. Spend as much intentional time in His presence as you can. I believe that your life ultimately is a reflection of your time spent in His presence.

Love Him with all of your heart, soul, and mind. Then, respond to His call. Seek Him first, and the rest will be added. There's no better place to dwell than in His presence. There's no greater gift than to know Him more.

> Jesus replied: "'Love the Lord your God with all your heart and with all your soul and with all your mind.' This is the first and greatest commandment."
>
> **Matthew 22:37–38**

PRAYER: Jesus, help me to prioritize my pursuit of You. Transform me into Your likeness as I spend time in Your presence. Amen.

REFLECTION/APPLICATION: Take some time to reflect on where you spend your time, who you spend your time with, and what you spend your time doing. What do you need to exchange or spend less time doing in order to spend more time pursuing Jesus and becoming more like Him?

HEAVENLY PERSPECTIVE

"For my thoughts are not your thoughts,
neither are your ways my ways,"
declares the Lord.
"As the heavens are higher than the earth,
so are my ways higher than your ways
and my thoughts than your thoughts."

Isaiah 55:8–9

God's power is not limited by your perspective. Your perspective cannot change this truth, but this truth can change your perspective.

MY SINCERE BELIEF that God's ways are better than my ways has transformed my life. Heavenly perspective allows us to entrust every unknown in our lives to an all-knowing God who is always working for the good of those who love Him. It invites us to live in confidence that He can see far beyond what we can see, that He knows far more than our minds can comprehend, and that the way He works is far greater than we can imagine. He can be nothing less than good.

This perspective has allowed me to celebrate when things don't go my way, even when it's painful, because I know that He sees far beyond the pain of the present moment. It has allowed me to submit my limited thoughts to the truth of His Word. It has caused me to surrender my plans to the One who knows it all, is in control of it all, and has my best interests at heart. There is no one who knows what is best for you like the One who knows you best, the One who calls you by name.

Our perspective of our circumstances will never change God's sovereignty and power, but His sovereignty and power will completely transform our perspective about our circumstances—and life in general—if we will allow them to.

Your present circumstance cannot change the truth of who God is, but who God is changes everything about your present circumstances (even the most devastating ones), in the very best way.

Having a heavenly perspective is fixing your eyes on eternity. It reminds us that God is ultimately in control and that our lives

> Your present circumstance cannot change the truth of who God is.

are so much bigger than the moment we're living in right now. Whatever you are facing today, know this: (1) God is sovereign and in control over everything in heaven and on the earth, and (2) your life is bigger than the brief time you spend on earth.

He has been faithful, He is faithful, and He will keep being faithful in your story. That's all you really need to know to hold on to hope.

> I have seen the burden God has laid on the human race. He has made everything beautiful in its time. He has also set eternity in the human heart; yet no one can fathom what God has done from beginning to end.
>
> **Ecclesiastes 3:10–11**

PRAYER: Jesus, change my perspective to see things more like You do. Help me to live in the confidence that Your thoughts and ways are higher than my own and that You are in control. Amen.

REFLECTION/APPLICATION: In what ways does the reality of eternity change your perspective of the present things you are facing? What evidence have you seen that God's thoughts and ways are higher than your own?

DAY 15

FAITH

Now faith is the substance of things hoped for, the evidence of things not seen.

Hebrews 11:1 NKJV

It is impossible to please God without faith. Don't live by what you see; live by what He says.

SCRIPTURE TELLS US that without faith, it is impossible to please God. Faith is much bigger and more important than a word on a T-shirt or in your Instagram bio. It isn't cliché; it is the very foundation of what we claim to believe as Christ followers. We have to learn to live it out if our desire is to honor God.

Faith requires us to believe as fact what we can't always see or feel. It requires us to trust what God said over what we can currently see. In our own understanding, it makes no sense, but it is an invitation to trust that His ways are higher and greater than we can comprehend. Faith is an opportunity to see Him be

> Faith requires us to believe as fact what we can't see or feel.

who only He can be and do what only He can do. It makes a fool of what makes sense in our own understanding.

I believe faith is required to please God because faith requires us to trust in Him. If there is anything you will learn as you continue to walk with Jesus, it's that He desires your wholehearted trust.

Faith causes us to believe that God is faithful, even through disappointment, unknowns, and the unexpected. Faith enables us to hold fast to every word God has spoken, not what the world around us is saying. Faith helps us to decide that God's goodness is not based on circumstances but simply on who He is. Faith leads us to surrender our fear of the future into the hands of One who is sovereign over all things.

I like to say it this way: Faith trusts that God sees the full picture when all I see is what is in front of me.

When what you see contradicts what God said, go with what He said, every time. Trust what He says to be true, even when you don't see the evidence at the moment. I can assure you of this—His Word will not return void.

He is still the God who moves mountains with mustard seed faith.

He replied, "Because you have so little faith. Truly I tell you, if you have faith as small as a mustard seed, you can say to this mountain, 'Move from here to there,' and it will move. Nothing will be impossible for you."

Matthew 17:20

PRAYER: Jesus, help me to trust what You have said over what I see at this moment. Show me areas in my life where You are calling me to trust You. Amen.

REFLECTION/APPLICATION: How does faith change your response when what you see contradicts what God says? How does the fact that God sees the full picture change your perspective about your current circumstance(s)? Write a list of some things you are believing Him for that you have not yet seen come to pass.

DAY 16

"FOLLOW ME"

As Jesus was walking beside the Sea of Galilee, he saw two brothers, Simon called Peter and his brother Andrew. They were casting a net into the lake, for they were fishermen. "Come, follow me," Jesus said, "and I will send you out to fish for people." At once they left their nets and followed him.

Matthew 4:18–20

Jesus's invitation is the same today as it was to the first disciples: to follow Him. Give Him your wholehearted yes! Every day, you are one day closer to the kingdom of heaven.

A S I WAS STUDYING THE GOSPELS, specifically Jesus's life and ministry on earth, these verses in Matthew 14 captured my attention and grabbed my heart like never before. It was as if He was talking to me through the page. Jesus's invitation to the disciples was simple—to follow Him. I love that it says the disciples' immediate response (not just in words but in action) was yes.

My heart is stirred with the reality that His invitation to you and me is the same today—to follow Him. He has called us to be disciples and to make disciples. The reward remains the same— fruitfulness as we are made fishers of men, because the kingdom of heaven is coming. We don't know when, but we get closer every day. There is no greater reward than carrying the eternal hope of heaven and seeing people come alive in the light of who Jesus is.

His invitation hasn't changed but our response is up to us. Will we give Him our wholehearted yes? There is an urgency we are called to live with as believers, to live lives that are full, faithful, and fruitful. We aren't here to just live and die; we are here to follow His lead, to be disciples (followers of Christ).

Yield to His instruction today and every day. Walk in the authority you have been given in and through Him to accomplish the unique purpose He has created you for, for His glory. Live a life that tells of who He is. Seek Jesus first. It will look different in each one of our lives, but we are all called to follow Him. His glory is the purpose for which each and every one of us was created.

What would it look like if we all gave Him our yes? I believe that His light would pierce through the darkness in our families,

> We aren't here to just live and die;
> we are here to follow His lead.

churches, neighborhoods, cities, nations, and world like never before. There should be nothing we want more than to know Jesus and for those around us to know Him.

He is the hope that wakes hearts up. It's time to be His hands and feet.

> To this you were called, because Christ suffered for you, leaving you an example, that you should follow in his steps.
>
> · **1 Peter 2:21**

PRAYER: Jesus, help me daily to respond yes to Your invitation to follow You in words and in action. Thank You for the opportunity to be Your hands and feet. Amen.

REFLECTION/APPLICATION: What hinders you from wholeheartedly following Jesus? How can you live more like the kingdom of heaven is near?

ESTABLISHED

Commit your work to the LORD,

and your plans will be established.

Proverbs 16:3 ESV

If we commit whatever we do to the Lord, He will be faithful to establish our steps. Release control and trust that His way is better.

THE PHYSICAL AND SPIRITUAL are in a constant battle in our lives. One example of this is the way in which we decide to make our plans. Our human nature is constantly trying to convince us that we need more control over our lives in order to be successful. It tells us that in order to succeed, we have to work more, try harder, and do better. Our own hearts and minds mislead us into believing that we are in charge of making our own plans and establishing our own steps. The reason I say mislead is because the One who knows what is best for us has a better plan.

God's Word instructs us to simply surrender. We are called to commit whatever we have and whatever we do to Him. He reminds us through His Word that He is in charge and in control of orchestrating His plans for each one of our lives, leading us step by step. It's up to Him to establish our lives.

There is nothing wrong with hard work. In fact, we are called to work hard. But it's not working harder that ultimately gets us where we are going. The success of those who follow Jesus is determined by their willingness to yield their lives to His instruction. We are called to live in confident trust that His plan is ultimately best for us and that He is responsible to get us where we need to be when we need to be there (even if it's different from our own plan).

When we don't know Him and trust His character, we may be misled to believe He is stealing our freedom. The more we trust Him, learn His heart for us, and understand His sovereignty, the more we come into awareness that there is so much freedom and security in surrendering our lives to the One who sees and knows it all. It takes so much pressure off us when we yield our lives to the One who holds the whole world in His hands. He is so faithful to exceed our expectations.

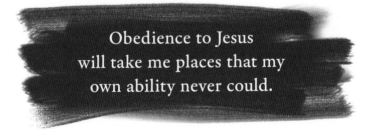

Obedience to Jesus will take me places that my own ability never could.

I like to put it this way: obedience to Jesus will take me places that my own ability never could.

That truth is the same for you as well. Commit whatever you do to Jesus today, and trust that He is unraveling His perfect plan for your life day by day and step by step.

> Your word *is* a lamp to my feet
> And a light to my path.
>   **Psalm 119:105 NKJV**

PRAYER: Jesus, help me to commit everything I do to You as I trust You to establish my every step. Thank You for having a plan for my life that is better than my own. Amen.

REFLECTION/APPLICATION: How does God's instruction to succeed contradict the world's instruction to succeed? What do you need to release control of and surrender to God so that He can establish your steps?

EQUIPPED FOR THE CALL

By his divine power, God has given us everything we need for living a godly life. We have received all of this by coming to know him, the one who called us to himself by means of his marvelous glory and excellence.

2 Peter 1:3 NLT

He is Jehovah Jireh, the One who provides. Not only does He provide but He is also faithful to show up at the right time on behalf of those who put their hope in Him.

ONE OF THE MOST detrimental lies you can believe is the lie that you are unequipped to be who God has called you to be and to do what He has called you to do. Too often, people count themselves out or give up because they feel inadequate or unqualified.

> Your good Father has not called you
> to do anything you can't do with His
> power at work in and through you.

You aren't qualified because of who you are; you are qualified through the One who has called you to Himself and chosen you. Your good Father has not called you to do anything you can't do with His power at work in and through you. Without Him, you would be hopeless, but in Him, you have everything you need to accomplish all He has prepared for you.

You are called first to have a relationship with Him. As you get to know the One who has called you more and more, your confidence in His ability to complete the good work He has started in you will increase more and more. It's not about who you are; it's about who He is. That's why self-doubt can't steal your calling from you if you don't allow it to.

His strength never runs out and He is your strength.

His power never runs out and His power is at work within you.

His authority never runs out and He has given you His authority.

His goodness never runs out and it's running after you.

His resources never run out so you will never be left without what you need.

His Word never fails and it is the guide of your life.

Not only does He always show up but He always shows up at the right time on behalf of those who put their trust in Him.

You are equipped for the call by the One who called you, and He won't fail you.

> All Scripture is God-breathed and is useful for teaching, rebuking, correcting and training in righteousness, so that the servant of God may be thoroughly equipped for every good work.
>
> **2 Timothy 3:16–17**

PRAYER: Jesus, help me to recognize that my qualification to be who You have called me to be and do what You have called me to do is found in You. Thank You that in You I have everything that I need. Amen.

REFLECTION/APPLICATION: How have feelings of insignificance or inadequacy affected the way you have responded to God's call on your life? How does His strength help you to overcome those feelings?

DAY 19

PATIENT ENDURANCE

Patient endurance is what you need now, so that you will continue to do God's will. Then you will receive all that he has promised.

Hebrews 10:36 NLT

Remember that faithfulness isn't about the reward, it's simply about God deserving our continual yes. Although He does promise abundance to those who patiently endure in doing His will.

GOD'S PROMISES often require our patience.
The fulfillment of God's plan is a process.
This process is not without pain, but the pain is never without purpose.
There will be moments, days, months, and maybe even years that it will feel like you are going nowhere fast. Remember that

your feelings don't always tell the truth; they are fleeting. There will be times that all you have left to cling to is His Word, and yet it will always be enough. Hold fast to what He said and don't let go. Sometimes the reward of your obedience will simply be knowing that you are giving Jesus what He is worthy of, and that's enough.

It's in those times of trial, doubt, and disappointment that the ability to press on is being produced within you. That leads you to receive the fullness of His promise. You get to choose if you will trust what you see or what He said. You get to choose daily whether or not you will take Him at His word. It won't always be easy, but it is always attached to an eternal reward.

He always means what He says, but you have to live a life of following His lead to find out. He hasn't brought you this far to forsake you. He leads you with kindness and intentionality. When He takes you the long way, rest assured that His way is the better way. When the timing is different than you expected, remember that He can accomplish more in a moment than you can in a lifetime. When it looks like your story will end in disappointment, remember that He sees the full picture when all you see is the right now.

Give Him your yes and live a life of faithfulness to Jesus, not just a moment here or there.

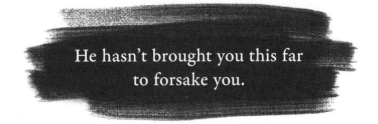

He hasn't brought you this far
to forsake you.

Don't strive with an ulterior motive of what more you can gain, but live in submission to His Word because He deserves your yes. Press on to see the fulfillment of His promise but remember that there is no greater reward than honoring the One who gave you abundant life. He is your strength to carry on.

> But as for you, be strong and do not give up, for your work will be rewarded.
>
> **2 Chronicles 15:7**

PRAYER: Jesus, help me to choose faithfulness over striving. You deserve my continual yes. Amen.

REFLECTION/APPLICATION: After reading today's devotion, what would you say is the reward of patient endurance? How does that reward help you to overcome the temptation to quit when you face doubt and discouragement?

DAY 20

PERFECT PEACE

You will keep in perfect *and* constant peace *the
one* whose mind is steadfast [that is, committed
and focused on You—in both inclination and
character],
Because he trusts *and* takes refuge in You
[with hope and confident expectation].

Isaiah 26:3 AMP

Peace is not found in knowing what comes next. Peace
is knowing Jesus in the midst of whatever comes and
goes. No matter what changes throughout your life, He
will remain.

I F YOU ARE ANYTHING LIKE ME, you struggle with the
temptation to find peace in the knowledge of what comes
next or your ability to control your life. The problem with that
mindset is that life doesn't always go according to our plans.
We don't have the control we like to think we do. If you place

PEACE is not knowing
what comes next.
PEACE is knowing Jesus.

your security in your own understanding, you will find yourself
in continual patterns of anxiousness and overwhelm when you
face the unknown or unexpected. I'm not saying having a plan
is wrong; I am saying that true peace can't be rooted in your
own plan.

PEACE is not knowing what comes next.

PEACE is knowing Jesus.

He is the only source of true peace.

You and I will never know peace as long as our assurance is
attached to our knowledge of the future or fleeting things. Peace
remains when plans change. Your security is not in having it all
figured out but in the One who has ordered your steps and who
promises to never leave you or forsake you along the way. Life
will often look different than you dreamed, hoped, or expected,
but God will never change and His plan is always better than
your own.

You can face the wildest unknowns and have complete peace
in Jesus when you are walking with Him. Peace is not found in
feelings or circumstances. Peace and joy are found in Him alone.
Knowing Jesus doesn't always mean knowing what comes next,
but it does mean having confidence in how the story ends, no
matter what the journey of arriving there looks like.

Decide that you would rather know Jesus than anything the world can offer you. Peace in Jesus can't be stolen from you because it is found in the unchanging and everlasting Prince of Peace Himself. Know Him, keep your gaze fixed on Him, and live in the security of trusting His perfect plan.

> Now may the Lord of peace himself give you peace at all times and in every way. The Lord be with all of you.
>
> **2 Thessalonians 3:16**

PRAYER: Jesus, help me to find my peace in who You are and the promise that Your way is better. Thank You that my security is in You and not in life going according to my own plans. Amen.

REFLECTION/APPLICATION: What is the difference between the peace Jesus provides and the peace we try to find in anyone or anything else? How does knowing Him as the Prince of Peace change our response to life going differently than we planned or expected?

THE COST OF COMPROMISE

So get rid of all the filth and evil in your lives, and humbly accept the word God has planted in your hearts, for it has the power to save your souls.

But don't just listen to God's word. You must do what it says. Otherwise, you are only fooling yourselves.

James 1:21–22 NLT

What God speaks will never contradict the truth of His Word. Don't allow impatience to cause you to compromise while you wait for His best for your life.

ONE OF THE MOST detrimental attacks to living your life with wholehearted trust in Jesus is becoming comfortable with compromise. Even a little compromise when it comes to your walk with Jesus is costly. He calls us to exchange our pursuit of what the world has to offer for the pursuit of Him. Both aren't an option because they are opposite in nature. He gives what the world never could. It's important to live in awareness of this reality.

Everything you do either draws you closer to Jesus or distances you from Him. Everything you do represents darkness or light. Be careful not to justify what separates you from Him. Consider who and what you are representing before you make a decision. To live in continual patterns of sin is to run back again and again to what Jesus died to save you from.

As you grow in your relationship with Jesus, your desire to honor Him should overwhelm the temptation to compromise or water down the truth of His Word. The more you understand His heart and His character, the more you will see that everything He instructs is purposeful and intentional. It's for your good and His glory.

When temptation creeps in, keep your eyes fixed on the promise of who He is. Don't allow impatience, peer pressure, loneliness, fear, doubt, or confusion to cause you to settle for less than His standard when it comes to your life. Remember that a good thing isn't always a God thing and keep following the sound of His voice.

> Everything you do either
> draws you closer to Jesus or
> distances you from Him.

If saying yes to your own desires requires you to compromise what He says in His Word, the cost is too great.

> You were running a good race. Who cut in on you to keep you from obeying the truth? That kind of persuasion does not come from the one who calls you. "A little yeast works through the whole batch of dough."
>
> **Galatians 5:7–9**

PRAYER: Lord, help me to not just listen to Your Word but to do what it says too. Increase my desire to honor You in all that I do. Amen.

REFLECTION/APPLICATION: After reading today's devotion, what would you say is the danger of becoming comfortable with compromise? Invite God to identify areas of compromise in your life and correct them through the truth and standard of His Word.

DAY 22

PURPOSE

For we speak as messengers approved by God to be entrusted with the Good News. Our purpose is to please God, not people. He alone examines the motives of our hearts.

1 Thessalonians 2:4 NLT

When we live to please people, satisfaction lasts for a moment. When we live to please God, the effect is everlasting.

PURPOSE IS DEFINED as the reason for which something (or someone) is created or exists. You need to know that your purpose is not your vocation. Your purpose is not to be a spouse or even to be a parent. Your purpose can't be found in your friendships, relationships, gifts, or passions. All of these things can be a part of fulfilling your purpose, but they aren't the reason you exist or what you should ultimately live for or search for satisfaction in.

> Your purpose, the reason
> for which you were created,
> is to display God's glory.

Your purpose, the reason for which you were created, is to display God's glory. You were created to know Him and to follow Him.

No matter what you accomplish in this lifetime, the greatest titles you will ever carry are "child of God" and "messenger of His Good News." These titles will require you to live for His "well done" instead of the applause of people. Your true purpose will require you to live willing to be misunderstood in order for His kingdom to move forward on earth as it is in heaven.

When you find yourself feeling insignificant, behind, consumed with comparison, or questioning your purpose, consider your Creator. He doesn't create useless or purposeless things. It's not in His nature. You are no exception. You are uniquely created in His image and for His glory.

Don't search for satisfaction in earthly titles, positions, or success. All of these things will keep you empty and searching. Rest secure in your eternal kingdom purpose to share the good news of the gospel. Wherever you find yourself and whatever you find yourself doing in this lifetime, do it with a sincere heart for God's glory. He sees you and knows your heart.

As long as you hold on to your own plan and preference with a white-knuckle grip, you won't experience the fulfillment of His plans and promises for your life. Exchange your plans for your desire to honor Him.

There is no greater purpose to live for. There is no greater reward than His "well done."

> Many are the plans in a person's heart,
> but it is the Lord's purpose that prevails.
> **Proverbs 19:21**

PRAYER: Jesus, help me to share the Good News with boldness and with a heart to please You. Remind me that my ultimate purpose is living for Your glory. Amen.

REFLECTION/APPLICATION: What are the differences between living for the world's approval and living to honor God? What personal preferences and plans is He asking you to let go of so that He can fulfill His plan for your life?

DAY 23

INCREASE
+ DECREASE

He must become greater and greater, and I must become
less and less.

John 3:30 NLT

Live for God's glory alone, not your own. In a culture
that is chasing the applause of humanity and is never
satisfied, seek His approval alone.

THE WAY YOU LIVE is a reflection of who and what you
live for. When it comes to your life, may your purpose be
undeniably clear. There should be no confusion about the God
you serve because the way you live lines up with His Word. Don't
complicate what has been made simple just because it's chal-
lenging. Don't make cloudy what He has made clear.

The purpose of our lives as followers of Jesus is not our own
gain but His glory. Be willing to decrease so that Jesus can in-

> The purpose of our lives
> as followers of Jesus
> is not our gain but His glory.

crease. If you are living for Him, you must be willing to die to yourself daily. Your life should and will contradict what the world is doing and pursuing in every way. When you give your life to Jesus, you exchange the pursuit of personal gain for kingdom purpose, and your life should be clear evidence of that exchange. Personal gain may satisfy for a moment, but it's fleeting. Kingdom purpose is eternal. Live for what lasts today and every day.

He is worthy of everything. He is the best gift we could ever be given and the best gift we have to offer to others. Every good thing about you is because of Him. Continually tell others of His goodness.

Your life should simply be a testimony of who He is and what He has done.

It should be a billboard pointing others His direction, not just when people are watching but even in the most mundane moments.

Don't live for Him to receive more from Him; live for Him because of what He has already done. He has saved you, He has freed you, and He calls you His own. Experience the abundance of living to see His kingdom come and His will be done on earth as it is in heaven. You won't always get it right, but He knows

your heart and will honor your sincere desire to live wholeheartedly for His glory.

Live in continual response to who Jesus is and what He has
done. You were made for His glory, not your own.

> Am I now trying to win the approval of human beings, or of
> God? Or am I trying to please people? If I were still trying to
> please people, I would not be a servant of Christ.
>
> **Galatians 1:10**

PRAYER: Jesus, I pray for Your kingdom to come and
Your will to be done through me. Help me to live contin-
ually in response to who You are and all You have done.
Amen.

REFLECTION/APPLICATION: Why does living for
personal gain ultimately leave us empty? How does living
for God's glory challenge the current culture we live in?

DAY 24

EVERY WORD

In the beginning was the Word, and the Word was with God, and the Word was God. . . . The Word became flesh and made his dwelling among us. We have seen his glory, the glory of the one and only Son, who came from the Father, full of grace and truth.

John 1:1, 14

God is His Word. His Word can't fail because He can't fail.

FAILURE IS NOT in God's nature. I remember when this truth changed my perspective forever. The awareness that God is His Word should increase our love for and desire to know and obey His truth. Our love for His Word and the way we apply it is a direct reflection of our love for Him. Scripture is active, alive, and will never return void. If we hold fast to what He has spoken, it will prove true every time.

If there is one thing you gain from this entire devotional, I pray it is a greater confidence in the trustworthiness of God's character because the more you trust Him, the bolder you will become in following Him. Pursuing Him is what you are made for. The enemy wants nothing more than to derail you from living like God's Word is true because it threatens his plan to steal, kill, and destroy. Victory over consuming lies is found in confidence in what God says. The solution to every problem and answer to every question is found in its pages and through the guidance of the Holy Spirit.

God doesn't speak empty words like people often do. He delivers. He follows through.

Living in obedience to God's Word results in His promises being fulfilled in our lives. When we trust His leadership, we will not be misled. When we put our hope in His Word, we don't have to fear the days ahead because He will direct us. There is no greater guide than the voice of the One who created us and calls us His own. He faithfully guides us step by step.

In the beautiful unraveling of God's plan for our lives, there is a real enemy who wants nothing more than to destroy and disrupt the process. Truth is your protection when the lies get

There is no greater guide than the voice of the One who created us and calls us His own.

loud. Establish His Word as the reigning authority in your life daily and His plan for you will prevail.

> God is not human, that he should lie,
>   not a human being, that he should change his mind.
> Does he speak and then not act?
>   Does he promise and not fulfill?
>
> **Numbers 23:19**

> Every word of God proves true.
>   He is a shield to all who come to him for protection.
>
> **Proverbs 30:5 NLT**

PRAYER: Jesus, help me to remain anchored in Your truth. Thank You for the promise that Your Word never fails. Amen.

REFLECTION/APPLICATION: How does the fact that God is His Word change the way you view it? How does our belief that God fulfills every word He speaks threaten the enemy's plan to steal, kill, and destroy God's abundant plan for our lives?

DAY 25

FULLNESS OF JOY!

You make known to me the path of life;
in your presence there is fullness of joy;
at your right hand are pleasure forevermore.

Psalm 16:11 ESV

Full and complete joy is your portion in Jesus. Remain continually in His presence and receive the promise of the fullness of joy.

YOU CAN BE JOYFUL but unhappy. Happiness is a surface-level emotion that is often determined by circumstances. Joy is deeply rooted and remains constant even in the face of changing circumstances.

Emotions fluctuate but joy is anchored in who Jesus is. It is found in Him alone.

Joy is not determined by what you have, so it can't be taken away because of what you lack.

> He is, He has always been,
> and He will always be good.

Joy is not found in where you are, so it can't be stolen when you find yourself in less-than-ideal places.

Joy is not found in your circumstances or situations, so it can't be robbed when you face heartbreak, hardship, or trial.

Since God never changes, your joy can remain unwavering when it's in Jesus.

It's constant because He is constant.

The test of true joy is in the trial. Joy proves steadfast through pain and still remains through the less-than-ideal circumstances of life.

This is another example of the way pain is repurposed in our lives to produce something priceless. There are countless examples of people in the Bible who had sincere joy in the face of devastating circumstances because of Jesus. Your life can be a similar example to the world around you that through Jesus alone, joy can be found in the most unlikely places and in the face of the most unexpected circumstances.

In order for your life to be a well of overflowing joy, it has to have depth. It has to be rooted in complete confidence in His goodness no matter what comes and no matter what goes. It can't be dependent on fleeting things because its foundation is built on the only One who is unchanging.

He is, He has always been, and He will always be good.

He is leading you and His presence is with you, and the fullness of joy is a result of a life lived in awareness of these realities.

> These things I have spoken to you, that my joy may be in you, and that your joy may be full.
>
> **John 15:11 ESV**

PRAYER: Jesus, help me to find my joy in You. Thank You for remaining constant no matter what changes. Amen.

REFLECTION/APPLICATION: Identify a time in your life when you were unhappy but still had joy. How do trials prove the evidence of joy in our lives?

DAY 26

PRAY WITHOUT CEASING

Rejoice always, pray continually, give thanks in all circumstances; for this is God's will for you in Christ Jesus.

1 Thessalonians 5:16–18

> Choose not to complicate what has been made simple.
> Pray continually, for He hears and He answers.

WHEN TALKING ABOUT PRAYER, the best thing to do is to refer directly to what God's Word says about it. Unceasing prayer is God's will for your life. Prayer is not a religious obligation; it's the privilege we have been given to communicate with Jesus. We get to talk to Him, and it's not just a one-way conversation—He hears and He answers.

He never wants you to stop praying. He wants you to talk to Him about everything and invite Him into every detail of your life. He already knows those details, but He wants to hear from you personally because He cares about you. He chose to have a relationship with His children because He wanted to, not because He had to. I'm so glad He did. You can't have a relationship with someone you aren't communicating with. If you struggle with prayer, simply think of it as communication with your closest friend. If you don't know what to say, pray His Word. It will never fail.

It's overwhelming to think about praying without ceasing unless you see Jesus as your closest friend. He should be your first call, every time. He should be the One you go to first in every circumstance. Prayer shouldn't be your backup plan; it should be your plan A.

I challenge you to pray. Pray like you believe God's Word is true. Pray like you believe God is who He says He is. Pray bold prayers. Pray conversational prayers. Ask. Seek. Talk. Make your requests known. Thank Him. Peace is a direct result of prayer. Prayer and thankfulness are two of the best remedies for anxiety.

A consistent prayer life will transform your life. It is purposeful and powerful. God isn't after a performance when it comes to prayer, just like He isn't after a performance when it comes to relationship with you. He wants you, the real you. You don't have to formulate the perfect words; you simply have to approach Him with a sincere heart to know Him more.

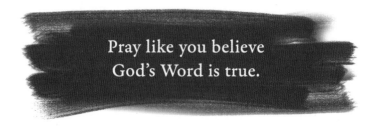

Pray like you believe
God's Word is true.

Last, I think it's important to remember that, wherever you are in your personal relationship with Jesus, when it comes to prayer, there is always room for more. Ask Him to take you deeper.

> Don't worry about anything; instead, pray about everything. Tell God what you need, and thank him for all he has done. Then you will experience God's peace, which exceeds anything we can understand. His peace will guard your hearts and minds as you live in Christ Jesus.
>
> **Philippians 4:6–7 NLT**

> Rejoice in hope, be patient in tribulation, be constant in prayer.
>
> **Romans 12:12 ESV**

PRAYER: Jesus, help me to live out Your will for my life when it comes to prayer. Thank You for choosing to have a relationship with me. Amen.

REFLECTION/APPLICATION: How does this perspective on prayer challenge your prayer life? Write out a simple, Scripture-based prayer.

DAY 27

THE HOLY TENSION OF TRUST

But blessed is the one who trusts in the LORD,
    whose confidence is in him.
They will be like a tree planted by the water
    that sends out its roots by the stream.
It does not fear when heat comes;
    its leaves are always green.
It has no worries in a year of drought
    and never fails to bear fruit.

Jeremiah 17:7–8

When we long to skip to the ending or even see three steps ahead, God allows us to live in the holy tension of the unknown and invites us to trust Him.

THERE HAVE BEEN many times throughout my life that I have found myself sitting in the tension of the unknown

> Every experience that deepens your
> trust in Jesus is for your good.

or unexpected. What I saw and what I was experiencing looked different from what I knew to be true or what God said. It has appeared at times as though what I was walking through was a punishment, but through continuing to allow Him to lead me, I've learned that trials are for my benefit.

Looking back, I truly thank Him for those experiences, because I see His intentionality woven through it all. That's the beauty of the journey.

If God showed us the full picture or answered us right away every time, it would require no faith in Him. The tension between what we see and what we know to be true about who God is and what He has promised us requires us to trust Him. The blessing in the unknown is an opportunity to trust Him. It's a holy tension. His Word says that those who trust confidently in Him are blessed. Every experience that deepens your trust in Jesus is for your good, even when it doesn't look or feel good in the moment. Psalm 112:6–7 is a great reminder:

> Surely the righteous will never be shaken;
>   they will be remembered forever.
> They will have no fear of bad news;
>   their hearts are steadfast, trusting in the Lord.

The burden can be a blessing. Your weakness is proof of His strength. Your lack is evidence of His provision. The tension is providing you with a story to tell of His faithfulness. The unknown and unexpected, if you yield to God's process, will lead you into a place of greater understanding of who He is. Put your trust in Him. He has a perfect track record of faithfulness.

> Trust in the LORD forever,
>   for the LORD, the LORD himself, is the Rock eternal.
>   **Isaiah 26:4**

PRAYER: Jesus, help me to trust You in the tension of the unknown. Thank You for every experience that has grown my trust in You. Amen.

REFLECTION/APPLICATION: Why is it a good thing that God doesn't reveal the future to us? How does following Jesus through the unknown increase our trust in Him?

OVERCOME THE WORLD

For everyone who has been born of God overcomes the world. And this is the victory that has overcome the world—our faith.

1 John 5:4 ESV

Your faith in God and your choice to follow Him lead to victory. Overcome the world by living out His Word!

YOU FIGHT DIFFERENTLY when you know the battle has already been won. I once heard it put this way, "You don't fight for victory, you fight *from* victory!" When it comes to the war between good and evil, the Bible tells us how the story ends. We are just living in the in-between. Jesus has already won the war and those who have put their trust in Him are on the winning side. We can live like the battle has already been won because it has been!

> The enemy is powerful
> but only God is all-powerful,
> and His power is at work
> within you.

The promise of victory is found in the One who has overcome the world.

We overcome the world through living a life of confident trust in God's Word. It is the greatest guide.

We are assured that we will face trials but we are also promised victory.

We may experience moments of defeat, but we won't be destroyed.

There will be times when it seems as though the enemy is rapidly gaining ground and darkness is closing in, but darkness cannot overcome the light no matter how things appear. We may feel consumed by temptation, but He always provides a way out.

He makes a way where there appears to be no way.

The enemy is powerful but only God is all-powerful, and His power is at work within you.

You are equipped to live an abundant life in the in-between. Just because you are equipped doesn't mean it will always be easy, but He is with you. The purpose of the right now isn't just to wait for what is to come. We are called to wait expectantly, but He has also instructed us to take action as we live in victory.

You are purposefully placed at this moment to tell others the good news of a Savior who has overcome the world. You are called to share the good news of the gospel wherever you go.

There is nowhere you can go that He hasn't gone before you. There is nothing unseen or unknown to Him. There is nothing you ask of Him that He can't accomplish. Don't live in fear of what's to come; live like the battle has been won.

Live like victory is yours in Christ.

> LORD, the God of our ancestors, are you not the God who is in heaven? You rule over all the kingdoms of the nations. Power and might are in your hand, and no one can withstand you.
>
> **2 Chronicles 20:6**

PRAYER: Jesus, help me to live like the battle is won! Thank You that my victory is in You. Amen.

REFLECTION/APPLICATION: What is the difference between fighting for victory and fighting *from* victory? What fears about the future should the promise of victory in Christ eliminate from your life?

DAY 29

THE REFINEMENT REQUIREMENT

I will bring that group through the fire
and make them pure.
I will refine them like silver
and purify them like gold.
They will call on my name,
and I will answer them.
I will say, "These are my people,"
and they will say, "The Lord is our God."

Zechariah 13:9 NLT

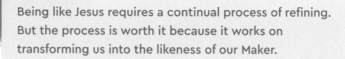

Being like Jesus requires a continual process of refining.
But the process is worth it because it works on
transforming us into the likeness of our Maker.

DID YOU KNOW that in order to become the precious and
rare metal it is, gold is put through fire and experiences

> He knows what He's doing
> and it's always for our good
> and for His glory.

great amounts of pressure? Its value increases the more it is put through because its impurities are burned away in the process. You and I are similar to gold in that way. In order for God's glory to be revealed in and through us in greater ways, we must go through a continual process of refinement to be transformed into His image.

Many claim they want to be like Jesus, but few are willing to yield their lives to the process of pruning (cutting away) that being like Him requires. In order to be like Him, the areas of our lives that don't look like Him have to be removed. No, the process is not painless, but the result is well worth it—to be transformed into the likeness of our Maker, the one who calls us His own and created us in His image and for His glory.

Will you answer His call today? Will you graduate from saying you want to be like Him and surrender to the process of refinement? When those around you catch a glimpse of your life, will it be undeniably clear whose image you reflect?

We can trust our Creator as He leads us through the fire knowing that He knows what He's doing and it's always for our good and for His glory. The process isn't punishment; even through the pain, it is full of purpose. There is no greater reward than knowing Him more and becoming more like Him.

He remains with us in the fire.

> See, I have refined you, though not as silver;
> I have tested you in the furnace of affliction.
> **Isaiah 48:10**

PRAYER: Jesus, help me to yield to the process of refining that will make me more like You today. Thank You that You are with me every step of the way. Amen.

REFLECTION/APPLICATION: What is a current area or thing in your life that doesn't reflect Jesus? How does today's devotion change your perspective about the refining process?

DAY 30

LIVE IN THE LIGHT

For once you were full of darkness, but now you have light from the Lord. So live as people of light! For this light within you produces only what is good and right and true.

Ephesians 5:8–9 NLT

> The Light of the World lives within you! Live in the Light so the world experiences the hope of who He is.

IF YOU GREW UP IN THE CHURCH, you probably remember singing the song "This Little Light of Mine" loud and proud. There's something about childlike faith that is so unashamed and precious in God's sight. The older we get, and the more aware we become of the world around us and of the thoughts and opinions of those around us, the more we tend to hide our light. What once seemed so obvious has become less clear. Where we were once bold, we're hindered. The light of Jesus living within us that once caused us to stand out in the darkness becomes hidden in the desire to blend in. We allow fear, insecurity, and doubt to keep the Light of the World to ourselves.

It's hard to admit, but we are quick to lose our wonder.

The truth is, Jesus has given you His light, but you get to choose whether or not you are going to let it shine. The truth is that the Light of the World lives within you, but you get to choose whether or not you will share Him with the world around you or keep Him hidden.

The truth is, He didn't call you out of darkness and into the light for you to live ashamed—you get to choose whether or not you will be bold and shine His light in dark places.

The truth is, your life is supposed to look different from the lives of those around you, but you get to choose whether or not you will live set apart.

The truth is, the world needs the light of Jesus, but unless you shine the light, the world will remain trapped in darkness.

You are not called to blend in or remain hidden; you are set apart and called to stand out. You are not created to follow the standard of the world; you are created to set the standard of the truth of God's Word to the world around you.

Live in the light. Let your light shine, not just because Jesus is worthy, but because those who don't know Him desperately need Him.

> He didn't call you out
> of darkness and into the light
> for you to live ashamed.

You are the salt of the earth. But if the salt loses its saltiness, how can it be made salty again? It is no longer good for anything, except to be thrown out and trampled underfoot.

Matthew 5:13

PRAYER: Jesus, help me to live in the light, set apart for Your glory. Thank You for Your grace when I've tried to hide Your light within me. Amen.

REFLECTION/APPLICATION: How does the physical contrast between darkness and light reflect the contrast between spiritual darkness and light? What has caused you to keep the light of Jesus within you hidden at times?

NUMBER OUR DAYS

Yet you do not know [the least thing] about what may happen in your life tomorrow. [What is secure in your life?] You are *merely* a vapor [like a puff of smoke or a wisp of steam from a cooking pot] that is visible for a little while and then vanishes [into thin air].

James 4:14 AMP

We don't get to choose or change the reality that our days on earth are numbered and that our time on this earth is limited. But we do get to decide what we do with our time and how we fill the fleeting days we are given.

IVE CONTINUALLY in the awareness of that reality. Not an awareness that cripples you with fear, but one that calls your faith into action. An awareness that doesn't make you want to look back and wish you would have made more of an eternal impact while you had the opportunity on earth.

What if we focused on making the most of what we can control rather than trying to change what we can't?

> In the timeline of eternity,
> we are only here
> for a short while.

I don't know about you, but I don't want to wait around for the comfortable and convenient moments to share the love of Jesus and the truth of His Word. That would make them few and far between. Instead, I desire to walk in the overflow of knowing a perfect Father and allowing Him to continually interrupt my ordinary life so that many see and know Him.

Don't allow your fleeting days to be consumed by fleeting, earthly things.

Fill them with what lasts forever—eternal things.

You may be in this world, but you are not of it.

It may be uncomfortable to stand out more times than not, but it's worth the discomfort.

Your feet may be planted on earth temporarily, but keep your eyes fixed on heavenly things. In the timeline of eternity, we are only here for a short while, but God can do mighty things in and through us for His kingdom in this short time if we surrender to His will. He desperately longs to use us for His glory.

Spend every moment you are given to share the best news of all time:

Jesus is alive! Heaven is home for those who confess, believe, and live like it is so. Don't keep this hope to yourself. Be the evidence of His goodness everywhere you go.

Teach us to number our days,
  that we may gain a heart of wisdom.
                              Psalm 90:12

PRAYER: Jesus, help me to live for what is eternal, not for what is fleeting. Thank You for strengthening me to live my days with intentionality for Your kingdom. Amen.

REFLECTION/APPLICATION: What does it mean to be in this world but not of it? How should our awareness that our days are numbered change the way we live our lives?

DAY 32

THE WAITING ISN'T WASTED

I waited patiently for the Lord;
    he inclined to me and heard my cry.
He drew me up from the pit of destruction,
    out of the miry bog,
and set my feet upon a rock,
    making my steps secure.

Psalm 40:1–2 ESV

The majority of your lifetime will be spent waiting for something. God's Word will strengthen you to embrace the waiting with hopeful expectation for Him to do what only He can do.

MOST OF YOUR LIFETIME will be spent in the waiting and in-between seasons. I call them the "meantime moments" of our lives. This is why the way we wait is so important.

We serve a God who wastes nothing, not even the waiting. There are good and necessary things produced within us as we wait for what comes next. While we wait, He strengthens us.

What stands out in Psalm 40 is David's heart of expectation. It's easy to become discouraged and frustrated when life isn't going how we hoped or planned, but it's more rewarding to wait full of hope and expectation for God to be who He is and to do what only He can do in and through our lives. Wait with confidence and patience instead of doubt and dread.

How we wait is a direct reflection of our trust in Jesus.

The more we trust Him through these moments, the more we grow in our trust in Him. The waiting doesn't mean that God has delayed His promise; it means He has purpose for where you are right now. Choose confident trust that He hears you and will come to the rescue of those who love Him every time. He is with you in the "meantime moments," and He is leading you through them.

Even and especially in the waiting, He is ordering your steps and keeping you steady. He is establishing His plan and purpose for your life. See the waiting not as a punishment but as a privilege. Through it, something valuable is being produced in you that otherwise couldn't be. Wait well. He is in control and working on your behalf.

> How we wait is a direct
> reflection of our trust in Jesus.

But those who wait for the LORD [who expect, look for,
    and hope in Him]
Will gain new strength *and* renew their power;
They will lift up their wings [and rise up close to God]
    like eagles [rising toward the sun];
They will run and not become weary,
They will walk and not grow tired.

Isaiah 40:31 AMP

PRAYER: Jesus, help me to wait with confident expectation, trusting that through it, You are producing something good within me. Thank You that no season in my life is wasted. Amen.

REFLECTION/APPLICATION: How has your perspective of "meantime moments" changed after reading today's devotion? What important things does waiting produce within you?

STILL WATERS + GREEN PASTURES

The Lord is my shepherd; I shall not want.
    He makes me lie down in green pastures.
He leads me beside still waters.
    He restores my soul.
He leads me in paths of righteousness
    for his name's sake.

Even though I walk through the valley of the
        shadow of death,
    I will fear no evil,
for you are with me;
    your rod and your staff,
    they comfort me.

You prepare a table before me
    in the presence of my enemies;
you anoint my head with oil;
    · my cup overflows.

Surely goodness and mercy shall follow me
    all the days of my life,
and I shall dwell in the house of the Lord
    forever.

Psalm 23 ESV

> Our awareness of who God is and what He has done renews our strength on the days we are convinced we can't take another step. He doesn't just lead us; He helps us carry on with joy for His glory.

I COULDN'T WRITE this devotional without including a day dedicated to this passage. In Psalm 23, God is revealed to us as our Good Shepherd. His Word describes us as the sheep of His pasture. If you look at this metaphor more closely, it's so profound. Some characteristics and responsibilities of shepherds are to guide, provide for, and protect their flock.

As your Good Shepherd, God guides, provides for, and protects you on this journey of living for Him day by day and step by step. He recognizes your need for renewal. He knows you—your every thought, fear, and frustration. He knows when you're exhausted, when your strength is running out and you're questioning if you can take another step.

He is intentional in His leadership. He goes before you, behind you, and surrounds you on every side. He doesn't just lead you; He strengthens you and guides you along the right paths. Everything He does is for your good and for His glory.

> Focus less on what's going on around you and more on the One who is leading you through it.

When you are overwhelmed, exhausted, afraid your strength is running out, or you don't know what step to take next, remember who your Shepherd is. Remember who your Provider is; remember who your Protector is. Focus less on what's going on around you and more on the One who is leading you through whatever you are faced with.

Peace in the chaos of life is found in Him. Rest in weariness is found in Him. Hope in hopelessness is found in Him. Provision in lack is found in Him. Clarity in confusion. Companionship in loneliness. Healing in heartache. The strength to carry on is found in Him.

Carry on today with confidence in the One who is leading you.

> Come to me, all you who are weary and burdened, and I will give you rest. Take my yoke upon you and learn from me, for I am gentle and humble in heart, and you will find rest for your souls. For my yoke is easy and my burden is light.
>
> **Matthew 11:28–30**

PRAYER: Jesus, strengthen me to carry on with joy for Your glory today. Thank You for Your perfect leadership. Amen.

REFLECTION/APPLICATION: In which area do you struggle to trust the Good Shepherd most—His ability to guide, to provide, or to protect? Why? How have you recently found rest in God's presence?

DAY 34

STEADFAST + IMMOVABLE

So, my dear brothers and sisters, be strong and immovable.
Always work enthusiastically for the Lord, for you know that
nothing you do for the Lord is ever useless.

1 Corinthians 15:58 NLT

The difference between steadfast faith and wavering
faith is that steadfast faith remains standing when the
storm comes. Its work is never in vain.

STEADFAST: *firm and unwavering, immovable*
Synonyms: loyal, faithful, committed, dedicated, dependable,
   reliable, true, constant, relentless, unchanging, unhesitating,
   uncompromising

IT'S GOING TO SOUND WEIRD but stay with me . . . Think
for a second about the fact that a tree's roots keep it planted.
You may not be able to see them, but they are vital to the life of
the tree in more ways than one. They provide nutrients to the

> ## The depth of your trust in God will be revealed when the storm comes.

tree and also keep it planted. The deeper the roots, the more likely the tree is to remain unmoved when the wind blows and the rain comes.

Faith is the root system of your spiritual walk with Jesus. The depth of your faith roots keeps you planted in the truth of God's Word in a life and culture that is constantly changing.

You are called to live a life of steadfast faith. It's not a suggestion; it's an instruction. The test of your faith is actually in what is unseen, not what is seen. Many appear to have it all together in the seen place, but the unseen place tells a different story. Jesus is most concerned with what your life looks like in the hidden places. The deeper your faith grows, the less easily moved you will be by the world around you. Storms will strengthen you.

Steadfastness is produced through the trial. The gift of God allowing you to experience storms in life is the opportunity for the roots of your faith to grow deeper. The true test of steadfastness is what remains when the winds of life blow and the rains of life fall. Remember the tree analogy.

The depth of your trust in God will be revealed when the storm comes. Know His Word and live His Word so that you are always prepared. The world will try to sway you. Be immovable.

Blessed is the one who perseveres under trial because, having stood the test, that person will receive the crown of life that the Lord has promised to those who love him.

James 1:12

PRAYER: Jesus, help me to hold fast to Your truth when my circumstances and the world around me are constantly changing. Thank You for producing steadfastness within me through the trials I face. Amen.

REFLECTION/APPLICATION: Spiritually speaking, if you were a tree, what would your root system look like right now? What disciplines can you put into place so that your roots of faith grow deeper?

EYES ON JESUS

Therefore, since we are surrounded by such a huge crowd of witnesses to the life of faith, let us strip off every weight that slows us down, especially the sin that so easily trips us up. And let us run with endurance the race God has set before us. We do this by keeping our eyes on Jesus, the champion who initiates and perfects our faith. Because of the joy awaiting him, he endured the cross, disregarding its shame. Now he is seated in the place of honor beside God's throne.

Hebrews 12:1–2 NLT

Keep your eyes on Jesus, for where your eyes are fixed will determine the course of your days. Don't be hindered by the distractions coming from every direction. God alone is worthy of your attention, even in the chaos of life.

THE WRITER OF HEBREWS compares our life of faith to a race set before us. Racing requires diligence, determination,

> In a world full of distractions,
> keep your eyes fixed on Jesus.

and continual focus on the end goal. Your focus determines your ability to finish what you started.

You have an easily distracted heart that is prone to wander and will continually be tempted to look in every direction. You are surrounded by distractions that will attempt to derail you from finishing the race set before you.

In this race, eternity is the reward, not an earthly prize. The enemy's best tactic is to trip you up in sin to get you to take your eyes off Jesus. If he can cause you to lose sight of the goal of eternity, he can get you to quit. If he can cause you to forget why you started and get your focus off the One whose strength is carrying you on, he can keep you from finishing.

Don't fall for his trap.

Don't look back except to tell of what Jesus has done.

Don't look to the right or to the left unless to reach out and invite people on this journey of faith with you.

The reward of this race is worth what it requires.

In a world full of distractions, keep your eyes fixed on Jesus.

You can't finish the race on your own, but if you keep your eyes on Jesus and rely on His strength, you will cross the finish line. He endured the cross for you; live your life for Him.

> I keep my eyes always on the LORD.
>   With him at my right hand, I will not be shaken.
> **Psalm 16:8**

PRAYER: Jesus, help me to fix my eyes on You. Thank You for empowering me to run welll the race set before me. Amen.

REFLECTION/APPLICATION: What distractions have caused you to take your eyes off Jesus? What does finishing the race that God has set before you require and why is it worth it to endure?

DAY 36

DON'T GROW WEARY

Let us not become weary in doing good, for at the proper
time we will reap a harvest if we do not give up.

Galatians 6:9

Things may not always look hopeful, but God is always
true to His Word. Don't lose heart in doing good for His
glory! It will be worth it if you press on.

THERE WILL BE MOMENTS in your walk with Jesus when
you feel overwhelmed with the temptation to quit. You will
experience discouragement and disappointment along the way.
The outcome of living for Him won't always be what you expect when you expect it. At times, what you see may appear to
contradict what He said. Remember that what you see doesn't
change what He said.

When you feel weary because of what you see, be strengthened by what you know to be true about who God is and what His Word says. His goodness isn't determined by how things seem, but by who He is. The fulfillment of God's promises isn't dependent on how things look or how you feel but on what He says. When you find yourself weary, cling to what He said, not how you feel or how things appear. He is always true to His word. Living according to what He said is the harder choice, but the reward is abundant for those who stay the course of doing good for His glory.

The difference between those who experience the harvest and those who don't is simply whether or not they keep following Jesus through every triumph, challenge, and mundane moment. God doesn't show partiality, but He does reward those who hold fast to His Word. Be the one who keeps following Him. When others quit, be set apart by your willingness to continue trusting that the Promise Keeper is leading you every step of the way. He has never not been faithful. He won't start with you.

You may not know all of what He has in store, but you can rest assured that it will be good. It may not be what you anticipated, but it will be what is best for you and what will most glorify God. He will lead you, He will strengthen you, and you will experience the reward of pressing on, just as He promised.

Don't lose heart.

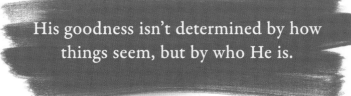

His goodness isn't determined by how things seem, but by who He is.

> Therefore, since through God's mercy we have this ministry,
> we do not lose heart.
>
> **2 Corinthians 4:1**

PRAYER: Jesus, when I'm weary, help me to be led by Your promise and not by how I feel. Thank You that my strength to carry on is found in You. Amen.

REFLECTION/APPLICATION: In what ways have your feelings misled you and tempted you to quit doing what God has called you to do? How does the promise of who He is and the promise in His Word encourage you to continue to follow Him even when it looks different than you hoped or expected?

ABUNDANTLY MORE

Now to him who is able to do far more abundantly than all that we ask or think, according to the power at work within us.

Ephesians 3:20 ESV

Our hope is in a God who is able to do abundantly more than we even know how to ask for or imagine. His power is at work within us.

ONE OF THE BEST pieces of advice I've ever received was this: "Sometimes it's hard to let go of our favorite flower, but when we finally do, God turns around and gives us a whole bouquet."

These words were shared with me during a time of deep disappointment in my life. It's often been in seasons of disappointment that His glory has most been revealed to me. It was difficult to see what God was doing in the moment, but looking back, that advice has proven truer than I could have ever imagined. That's the thing about God, He is really good at being God. One of my favorite characteristics of Him is His ability to do abundantly more than we even know to ask for.

He wants to do in and through you what only He can do, but it will require you to relinquish control of your own expectations and yield to His way. You will have to exchange your desire for control with your confidence in His plan. You can't go where He wants to lead you if you won't let go of the white-knuckle grip you have on your own plans and expectations. You have to be led by your trust that His way is better.

The more you follow Jesus, the more you will expect Him to exceed your expectations. The more steps forward you take in confident trust in who He is, the more He will prove Himself faithful. Not because He has to but because He wants to!

Know this: God wouldn't ask you to let go of what you have if He didn't have something far better in mind. If you only knew what was on the other side of your surrender, your yes would be easy, but instead of telling you what is on the other side, He chooses to lead you step by step in order to increase your trust

> God wouldn't ask you to let go of
> what you have if He didn't have
> something far better in mind.

in and dependence on Him. Not only does He call you to surrender but He strengthens you to surrender.

Your own strength and ability will always fail you, no matter how hard you strive, but God's power at work within you equips you to live a life of obedience to His Word. Obedience leads to abundant life.

When your hands are shaky and your heart aches to let go of your way, remember that He keeps every promise He makes. You will look back and be so thankful you exchanged your "favorite flower" for the bouquet He has to offer.

Don't allow fear or anything else to keep you from experiencing the fullness of His plan and purpose for your life. Expect Him to exceed your expectations.

> And we know that in all things God works for the good of those who love him, who have been called according to his purpose.
>
> **Romans 8:28**

PRAYER: Jesus, help me to trust Your ability to exceed my expectations. Thank You that Your power is at work within me. Amen.

REFLECTION/APPLICATION: In what area of your life is God calling you to surrender control? How has He exceeded your expectations and proven His faithfulness to you?

IN HIS IMAGE, FOR HIS GLORY

So whether you eat or drink or whatever you do, do it all for the glory of God.

1 Corinthians 10:31

> Live for the glory of the One who created you in His image. He longs to do something unique through you for His name's sake.

IF I COULD GIVE each one of you and myself a gift, it would be the ability to see ourselves and one another the way Jesus does. I truly believe that would eliminate insecurity and comparison in our lives. The most beautiful and miraculous thing about you is the One in whose image you are created. You are not only created in His image but for His glory.

The way you were created (very much not limited to, but including, the way you look) reflects your Maker. That's the most beautiful and valuable thing about you—the Artist who designed you and the fact that you were made to reflect His likeness.

His Word is clear about His thoughts toward you, and He defines your value. His Word says:

YOU are priceless.

YOU are beautifully, intentionally, fearfully, and wonderfully made in His image.

YOU are precious in His sight, and He delights in you.

He knows everything about you and loves you unconditionally.

He doesn't look at you and think of all the things He wishes He would have done differently. Neither should you. He sees you as His own, a vessel through which His goodness and glory and beauty is revealed. He has filled you with purpose to further His kingdom on earth as it is in heaven.

God made no mistake when He made you. Mistakes are not in His nature, and you are no exception. The cure to insecurity, comparison, and feelings of inadequacy is NOT a change in who you are or how you look. To live in continual awareness of who He is and the truth of His Word is the answer. It's to celebrate the way you and those around you have been so uniquely and intentionally designed by God. It's to get to know what He says

> The most beautiful and miraculous thing about you is the One in whose image you were created.

about you and live like it's true, like you are the wonderful work of His hand. I understand that this is easier said than done, but it isn't impossible. Again, His Word is the answer.

Speak His truth over every insecurity until you're living like you really believe that what He says is true.

When you criticize yourself and others, you criticize not only His creation but His image.

It's hard to hear but we need to hear it.

We will all have our days, and His grace is sufficient for those days, moments, and thoughts.

On those days and in those moments, remember this—no matter what you wish you could change about yourself, you reflect the very image of God. There is nothing more beautiful or miraculous about you than that.

> Then God said, "Let us make mankind in our image, in our likeness, so that they may rule over the fish in the sea and the birds in the sky, over the livestock and all the wild animals, and over all the creatures that move along the ground."
>
> **Genesis 1:26**

PRAYER: Jesus, help me to see myself and others the way You do. I celebrate the way I am uniquely created in Your image and for Your glory. Amen.

REFLECTION/APPLICATION: Who and what have you tried to find your value in outside of Jesus? How should the fact that you are made in His image and for His glory change the way you view yourself and others?

FEAR NOT

So do not fear, for I am with you;
   do not be dismayed, for I am your God.
I will strengthen you and help you;
   I will uphold you with my righteous right hand.

Isaiah 41:10

Fear is a liar and a thief. God's truth is your weapon in combating debilitating fear in your life. He is with you and for you.

ONCE HEARD A QUOTE that completely changed my perspective. It said, "Fear doesn't prevent death; it prevents life." Fear will withhold you from living the abundant life Jesus came that you might have. The enemy comes only to steal, kill, and destroy, and fear is one of his greatest tactics. He wants you to waste your life by being so consumed with concern that you don't accomplish what God created you for.

> Don't give your fear of tomorrow authority to keep you from the promise Jesus has for you today.

It's amazing the things fear will hinder you from in this lifetime if you allow it to. I know firsthand. I spent many years of my life limited by it. I was afraid of failing, afraid of rejection, and afraid of what people might say or think.

I lived so afraid of tomorrow, it took up all of my current day. So many days.

Fear had its grip on me, and its grip was tight and suffocating.

It was a grip that only Jesus could free me from, and I'm so thankful that He did. I now spend my days in His freedom, following the sound of His voice. I'm living proof of His goodness, and I live to tell the story. I recognize that I wouldn't even be writing these words if fear had its way in my life.

Fear loses its power in the light of the truth. The One who instructs you to fear not today has the final say. If you take Him at His word, fear won't be your future. When He says He is with you, He means it. When He says He will strengthen you, He means it. When He says He will uphold you, He means it.

It doesn't mean you won't face moments of fear, but it does mean you will have an unshakable confidence in those moments that will carry you through them.

It means you can conquer fear instead of fear conquering you.

Don't give your fear of tomorrow authority to keep you from the promise Jesus has for you today. His plans are to give you hope and a future, and He will follow through.

> I sought the LORD, and he answered me;
> he delivered me from all my fears.
> **Psalm 34:4**

PRAYER: Jesus, help me to trust Your voice instead of the voice of fear in my life. Guide me in living the abundant life You came that I might have. Amen.

REFLECTION/APPLICATION: What is fear holding you back from? How has fear prevented you from living life abundantly? What lies has fear told you, and how does the light of truth expose those lies?

DAY 40

SERVANT OF ALL

Sitting down, Jesus called the Twelve and said, "Anyone who wants to be first must be the very last, and the servant of all."

Mark 9:35

The kingdoms of heaven and earth are entirely different. Being like Jesus and first in the kingdom of heaven requires a life of wholehearted servanthood.

IT'S PROFOUND, really, the way that the King of Kings arrived on earth. The Savior of the world, the Son of God, entered in as a baby in a manger. This was no accident or coincidence. The way He came set the precedent for the life He would live. If anyone deserved an arrival fit for a king, it was Jesus, yet He arrived humble and lowly. When He entered the world, everything changed.

The kingdom of heaven flips the world's way of doing things upside down. It exchanges a life of selfish ambition for a life of humble servanthood. Jesus didn't come to earth for His own glory or gain; He lived to fulfill the will of His Father. He walked

> Choosing to follow Jesus
> is signing up for a life
> of humble servanthood.

the earth with sincerity, authenticity, and humility. The life Jesus lived was a clear reflection of the purpose He claimed to live for. Nothing that He did was with selfish ambition; everything He did pointed people to His Father.

He wasn't seeking royal treatment; He was too busy serving.

He was a king who washed feet.

He was a king with sincere compassion for those the world had overlooked.

He was a king who fed the hungry, healed the sick, and raised the dead.

He was a king who preferred others over Himself.

He was a king who died for the redemption of His people.

Jesus proved that true leadership is servanthood.

What does this mean for us who are called to follow His example?

Choosing to follow Jesus is signing up for a life of humble servanthood. There is no loophole out of that reality. If the King of Kings and Savior of the world chose a life of humility, what is our excuse to choose our own pride?

Being first in the kingdom requires that we give up our desire to build our own kingdoms on earth for our calling to see God's kingdom come and His will be done on earth as it is in heaven.

Being first in the kingdom challenges us to recognize that we live for a cause that is much bigger than ourselves. We have to decide that what we can give and how we can serve others is more important than what we can gain. Instead of living a life accumulating earthly titles and treasures, live for a kingdom that will never be shaken.

Instead of living for your own glory or gain that has no eternal value, follow the example of the lowly king. If you want to be first in the kingdom, be a servant of all.

> In your relationships with one another, have the same mind-set as Christ Jesus:
>
> Who, being in very nature God,
>   did not consider equality with God something to
>   be used to his own advantage;
> rather, he made himself nothing
>   by taking the very nature of a servant,
>   being made in human likeness.
> And being found in appearance as a man,
>   he humbled himself
>   by becoming obedient to death—
>   even death on a cross!
>
> **Philippians 2:5–8**

PRAYER: Jesus, thank You for living a life of servant-hood. Help me to follow Your perfect example. Amen.

REFLECTION/APPLICATION: How is worldly success different from kingdom success? What is the significance of Jesus living a life of servanthood and why does He call us to live that way too?

THE ANCHOR OF YOUR SOUL

So God has given both his promise and his oath. These two things are unchangeable because it is impossible for God to lie. Therefore, we who have fled to him for refuge can have great confidence as we hold to the hope that lies before us. This hope is a strong and trustworthy anchor for our souls. It leads us through the curtain into God's inner sanctuary.

Hebrews 6:18–19 NLT

One of the greatest things about God's perfect character is that He cannot lie. The hope you have in Him is an immovable anchor for your soul.

WHEN YOUR HOPE IS IN JESUS, your story won't end in disappointment.

I've learned that the way I respond to disappointment in my life is a reflection of where I'm placing my hope. Disappointment is inevitable, it's painful, and oftentimes it will catch you off guard. But disappointment gives God an opportunity to prove His faithfulness. It gives you and me an opportunity to surrender our lives again and again into the hands of the One who is ultimately in control. It gives us an opportunity to trust that His plans are good despite what we may see or experience. Disappointment reminds us not to put our trust in what is fleeting and can fail.

If you place your hope in what you see, feel, or even experience, disappointment will consume your life. If you place your hope in Jesus, disappointment will simply deepen your trust in His goodness as you run to Him in the midst of pain and confusion. He will reveal Himself to you like never before when you cling to Him and keep your eyes fixed on Him through the challenges and trials you face.

You can actually respond to disappointment with rejoicing when your hope is in Jesus because of your confident trust that He is in control. When you live in awareness that He is equally faithful on your best and worst days, you always have a reason to worship.

You get to choose where you place your hope today, but it's only if you place your hope in Hope Himself that it won't end in disappointment. Everything and everyone else will fail you. Jesus's presence doesn't mean the absence of hardship, but His

> He was faithful, He is faithful, and He will be faithful.

presence is our unfailing and unchanging hope in the midst of every trial we walk through.

He was faithful, He is faithful, and He will be faithful.

You may not see the full picture on this side of heaven, but the story He is writing isn't over unless it's good. The world is watching how you respond; point them to the hope of Jesus.

> And hope does not put us to shame, because God's love has been poured out into our hearts through the Holy Spirit, who has been given to us.
>
> **Romans 5:5**

PRAYER: Jesus, help me to see disappointment in my life as an opportunity to trust You more. Thank You that You never change or fail. Amen.

REFLECTION/APPLICATION: What does it mean for hope to be the anchor of our souls? How does God reveal His faithfulness through disappointment?

DAY 42

THE NARROW
· ROAD

Enter through the narrow gate. For wide is the gate and
broad is the road that leads to destruction, and many enter
through it. But small is the gate and narrow the road that
leads to life, and only a few find it.

Matthew 7:13–14

His Word is clear when it says that the easier way in this
life isn't the better way. Enter the narrow gate. Stay on
the narrow path.

I LOVE THE TRAIL MIX ANALOGY when it comes to God's
Word. It's silly, but so true. God's Word isn't like a bag of
trail mix; you can't just pick out the parts you want to believe
in and apply.

There is only one absolute truth, and it is His Word. Too often
in my life, I have avoided telling people the truth out of fear of

> Lay down your preference
> at His feet and exchange it
> for His truth that leads to life.

hurting their feelings. I refuse to make the same mistake with you. When someone is being led astray by a lie, the most loving thing you can do is tell them the truth, even if it offends their way of doing things.

We aren't called to share and apply just the parts of His Word that are easy to hear and live out but the entirety of it. In Matthew 7, Jesus talks about two roads. One is wide and it leads to destruction and the other is narrow and it leads to life.

The uncomfortable truth is that what is easy is typically far less rewarding. This is certainly true when it comes to our spiritual lives. Following Jesus is not an easy road, but its reward is life. Following Jesus isn't the most popular path and it doesn't yield to your preference, but the reward is worth the cost of your preference. The destructive road may gain you popularity and allow you to live according to what you want in life, but it leads to death.

Sometimes your desires are leading you to death. The thoughts you are thinking and things you are doing may seem small and harmless, but if they are distancing you from Jesus, they are gradually leading you toward death.

Your place in heaven can't be earned by being a good person. Only those walking in sincere relationship with Jesus can enter in. Walking with Him is the narrow path that leads to life. Relationship with Him will transform you from the inside out. It will change your thoughts and desires. When you are walking with Him, don't fear making a mistake. He knows your heart and will lovingly correct you and keep leading you along the path of righteousness.

Lay down your preference at His feet and exchange it for His truth that leads to life. Be found among the few who find the narrow road and take others with you along the journey. Remain on the narrow road.

> Not everyone who says to me, "Lord, Lord," will enter the kingdom of heaven, but only the one who does the will of my Father who is in heaven. Many will say to me on that day, "Lord, Lord, did we not prophesy in your name and in your name drive out demons and in your name perform many miracles?" Then I will tell them plainly, "I never knew you. Away from me, you evildoers!"
>
> **Matthew 7:21–23**

PRAYER: Jesus, thank You for the entirety of Your Word. Help me to remain on the narrow road and to bring others along it with me. Amen.

REFLECTION/APPLICATION: What in God's Word has been a challenge for you to accept or apply? How does the analogy of the narrow road challenge and encourage you to follow Jesus in a way that leads others to follow Him too?

KNOWN BY LOVE

By this everyone will know that you are my disciples, if you love one another.

John 13:35

Aside from loving Jesus, loving people is the greatest commandment. Let His love within you be undeniable.

THERE ARE MANY THINGS you can be known for in this lifetime, but not one of them is more important than being marked by the love of Jesus. The undeniable evidence of His love within you is more important than anything else you will accomplish. Jesus's love is what made Him the most recognizable when He walked the earth, and it makes us most recognizable as those who follow Him. To love like He loves is not a suggestion; it is a command given to those who love Him. It's what sets His disciples apart from the world around them, including us today. The truth is that people won't see Jesus in you unless they see His love on display in your life.

We don't love because everyone deserves it; we love because we were loved first when we didn't deserve it.

Not only have we been given a command to love, but we have also been given a perfect example to follow. He doesn't just tell us what to do, He provides us a perfect example of how to do it through His own life and His Word. We aren't expected to do what He wasn't willing to do first.

Your life will be a reflection of those you spend the most time with. If you are going to be known by love, it will require you to spend the majority of your time with Love Himself. Spend time learning and living what His Word says about love. Too often, we complicate what His Word has made clear because it's uncomfortable to apply.

First Corinthians 13:4–7 says,

> Love is patient, love is kind. It does not envy, it does not boast, it is not proud. It does not dishonor others, it is not self-seeking, it is not easily angered, it keeps no record of wrongs. Love does not delight in evil but rejoices with the truth. It always protects, always trusts, always hopes, always perseveres.

This chapter goes on to say, "And now these three remain: faith, hope and love. But the greatest of these is love" (v. 13).

The word *always* in this passage points out that love isn't a feeling or a fleeting emotion but a choice we continually make. We don't love because everyone deserves it; we love because we were loved first when we didn't deserve it. Love is a lifestyle.

It is a lifestyle that requires that we lay down our lives daily, pick up our crosses, and follow Him (Matt. 16:24). It's not easy, but we have the perfect example in the One who gave up His own life because of His great love for us. Without love, everything amounts to nothing. Above all else, love.

> My command is this: Love each other as I have loved you. Greater love has no one than this: to lay down one's life for one's friends.
>
> **John 15:12-13**

PRAYER: Jesus, I pray that Your love would be undeniable in my life. Thank You for the example You have given me to follow. Amen.

REFLECTION/APPLICATION: How is Jesus's love different from worldly love? What are some ways you can share His love with those around you?

NO GOOD THING

For the LORD God is a sun and shield;
the LORD bestows favor and honor.
No good thing does he withhold
from those who walk uprightly.

Psalm 84:11 ESV

Many long for the promises of God but refuse to live obedient to His Word. Walk according to God's Word and no good thing will be withheld from you.

IF YOU ARE IN CHRIST TODAY, you live in the hope of this promise: He will withhold no good thing from you. There is a condition to living in the fullness of this promise though. You have to live in obedience to His Word and according to His instruction. Your responsibility is to trust and surrender, and His responsibility is to follow through on His Word. He always follows through, but you have to choose to live a life of following Him to find that out.

A good parent provides for their child but doesn't give them everything they want, because they recognize that everything they want isn't good for them. A good parent always has their child's best interest at heart and protects them from the danger that they can't see in certain requests, desires, and decisions. Because of their love, good parents say no sometimes.

God is an even better father than the very best earthly one. The truth is that everything you think is good for you isn't. Everything you ask Him for isn't what's best for you. Anything that hinders you from His will for your life isn't ultimately good. It may seem, look, or feel good according to your understanding, but He always has something better in mind. He operates with an awareness of every detail of your life; He doesn't miss a thing. Trust His answer to your asks and desires.

In His yes—He is loving, faithful, and good.

In His wait—He is loving, faithful, and good.

In His no—He is loving, faithful, and good.

Trusting Him as a good Father allows us to arrive at a place where we can thank Him that He doesn't give us everything we desire or do everything our way. Trust causes us to acknowledge that our plan and preference aren't what's best because our vision and understanding are limited. Trust leads us to live a life of surrender to the One who will never fail us. It positions us to

You don't have to live life in fear of lack or of missing out if you believe what His Word says is true.

continually live in the unraveling of His perfect plan and to be recipients of His promises.

He won't give you everything you want, but He will provide everything you need, and He is continually leading you along the path of His perfect plan for your life. He is always working behind the scenes for your good and for His glory. You don't have to live life in fear of lack or of missing out if you believe what His Word says is true.

You might not always understand what He is doing or why He is doing it. There will be times you will wish He would do something differently. When you find yourself disappointed in His answer or His way of doing things, remember the promise you are living in if you are living according to His Word: your good Father will withhold no good thing from you. Keep trusting Him.

> If you, then, though you are evil, know how to give good gifts to your children, how much more will your Father in heaven give good gifts to those who ask him!
>
> **Matthew 7:11**

PRAYER: Jesus, I thank You that You don't give me everything I desire or do everything my way because I trust that Your way is better. Help me to grow in confidence that You will always protect and provide for me. Amen.

REFLECTION/APPLICATION: Looking back on your life, how have you seen that God's plan is better for your life than your own? How have you seen His faithfulness in His yes, His wait, and His no?

DAY 45

EMBRACE

Consider it pure joy, my brothers and sisters, whenever you face trials of many kinds, because you know that the testing of your faith produces perseverance. Let perseverance finish its work so that you may be mature and complete, not lacking anything.

James 1:2–4

God uses the trials we face to grow us in our walk with Him. Embrace the trials you face, knowing that something necessary is being produced within you in the process.

GOD'S WORD wouldn't instruct us on how to face trials if a relationship with Him meant we would never encounter them. Walking with Jesus won't keep you from all trouble, but He will be your hope when trouble comes. In fact, His Word promises that you will face many trials, but more importantly, it promises

> Walking with Jesus won't keep you from all trouble, but He will be your hope when trouble comes.

His presence in the midst of every trial you face. You will never be abandoned or unprepared when they come.

Looking through the lens of God's Word allows you not only to expect but to embrace the trials you face in life and consider them joy. Your confidence in who He is and His ability to work all things together for good will allow you to find rest even in the face of the greatest challenges you face. The truth is, if you were protected from all trouble, you would miss so many important things that the process of walking through trials produces within you. Things like steadfastness, trust, and maturity in your faith.

Instead of taking away the problem, He will often lead you through it. This is because of His kindness and intentionality. He sees what you need much more clearly than you do, and He knows that there are depths of faith you will only reach when you are placed in circumstances and situations that require you to put your trust in Him. It won't always make sense, but He is always good.

You don't have to celebrate every hard thing that happens in your life, but you can always praise Him for who He is in the midst of those trials. You can rejoice in His faithfulness to produce good and necessary things within you in the process. The blessing in every trial will be found in your sincere trust that Jesus is faithful.

Your joy isn't circumstantial—it's in Jesus—so you can have joy in everything, because He never changes.

Today—choose to trust.

Today—embrace the joy in the trial.

> And the God of all grace, who called you to his eternal glory in Christ, after you have suffered a little while, will himself restore you and make you strong, firm and steadfast.
>
> **1 Peter 5:10**

PRAYER: Jesus, help me to embrace the trials I face because of my trust in Your faithfulness. Thank You for never changing and never failing. Amen.

REFLECTION/APPLICATION: What is something good that God has produced within you as a result of walking through a trial in life? How does that change the way that you will embrace momentary suffering?

DAY 46

MULTIPLY

"We have here only five loaves of bread and two fish," they answered.

"Bring them here to me," he said. And he directed the people to sit down on the grass. Taking the five loaves and the two fish and looking up to heaven, he gave thanks and broke the loaves. Then he gave them to the disciples, and the disciples gave them to the people. They all ate and were satisfied, and the disciples picked up twelve basketfuls of broken pieces that were left over. The number of those who ate was about five thousand men, besides women and children.

Matthew 14:17–21

> Jesus will use what seems small and insignificant to reveal His power. Give Him what you have, and He will do what only He can do with it.

I LOVE THE STORY of Jesus feeding the crowd of five thousand with five loaves of bread and two fish provided by a young boy (John 6:1–13). He used someone and something small and seemingly insignificant in the eyes of humanity to perform the impossible. As a result, His miraculous power was on display for many to see, and we are still reading and talking about it today.

What stands out to me and challenges me in this passage is the young boy's willingness to give what he had. It may not have seemed like much, especially compared to the crowd of hungry people standing in front of him, but it was something. Doubt made more sense in that circumstance, but faith makes a fool of what makes sense. God can do anything, but He chooses to use ordinary people to do extraordinary things in order to reveal His glory. He can do big, unimaginable things with our offering of a little, but we have to be willing to put it in His hands.

Many of us have heard this story countless times, but has it really become real to us? Have we really grasped that the God who fed five thousand people with five loaves and two fish is the same God at work within us at this moment in time? If so, do we live like it's true?

We are too quick to forget that God has the same ability today to use what seems small, insignificant, and mundane in our lives

> God can do anything,
> but He chooses to use ordinary
> people to do extraordinary things
> in order to reveal His glory.

to point people to Him. We pray for miracles yet often doubt His power and hold on to what we have with a white-knuckle grip.

He is looking for hearts that are willing to give what they have, no matter how small it may seem in their own eyes or even in the eyes of others. He is looking for sons and daughters who are confident in His ability, not their own, to do the miraculous through their surrender and their willingness to give what they have in order to see Him do it.

Each of us has an opportunity to live in daily surrender and to live lives full of His glory being made known because of it. We will experience many circumstances where doubt makes more sense, but again, faith makes a fool of what makes sense and will lead us to surrender.

You may not be able to do everything, but you can do something. What you have to offer may seem small, but it's plenty in the hands of the One whose resources are unlimited.

He wants to use you to reveal His miraculous power.

Give Him what you have and watch Him multiply it beyond your wildest dreams.

> "Bring the whole tithe into the storehouse, that there may be food in my house. Test me in this," says the LORD Almighty, "and see if I will not throw open the floodgates of heaven and pour out so much blessing that there will not be room enough to store it."
>
> **Malachi 3:10**

PRAYER: Jesus, thank You for using what seems small and insignificant to reveal Your power. Help me to give You what I have and trust You to do with it what only You can do. Amen.

REFLECTION/APPLICATION: How has feeling insignificant kept you from surrendering what you have to Jesus? How does the story of Jesus feeding five thousand challenge you to give Him what you have?

DAY 47

AN EMPTY TRADE

And what do you benefit if you gain the whole world but
lose your own soul? Is anything worth more than your soul?

Matthew 16:26 NLT

> The most important thing you have is life in Jesus. Don't
> gain the treasures of this world but lose what's most
> important.

THE WORLD MAKES many empty promises that it can't
deliver.

Jesus never makes a promise He can't or won't keep.

You are constantly being bombarded with the temptation to
trade an eternal hope and promise for a fleeting, earthly one.
To exchange your relationship with Jesus for earthly security,
success, or satisfaction is a cheap, sad, and empty trade. It will
never truly satisfy you because it's not what you were made for.

Every day there are people trading what they are made for,
for a fleeting moment or season of satisfaction (fame, fortune,

> If you lose everything you long for
> on earth but keep your eyes
> and your heart fixed on Jesus,
> you gain everything.

fun, the list goes on and on), and they have been doing so since the beginning of time. The world can't give you what only Jesus can, but it will always try to convince you that it can. Don't be deceived.

You were made to love and be loved by Jesus and to live for His glory. What the world has to offer you will never compare to what only He can give. Your Creator knows you completely, and His promises and plans for those who love Him are greater than anything this world has to offer.

If you gain everything you long for on this earth but lose sight of your First Love, you have lost everything. If you lose everything you long for on earth but keep your eyes and your heart fixed on Jesus, you gain everything.

When you give your life to Jesus, you trade what you want for what He has, trusting with confidence that He won't lead you astray. Don't be deceived; remain steadfast in trusting Him. Your desires dictate your life, so may your greatest desire be to know, trust, and follow Him. May you store up treasures in heaven that will last forever instead of on earth where they are quickly fleeting.

Trade earthly for eternal, not eternal for earthly. Jesus is the greatest treasure. He is the greatest prize. He is the greatest reward.

> Sell your possessions and give to the poor. Provide purses for yourselves that will not wear out, a treasure in heaven that will never fail, where no thief comes near and no moth destroys.
>
> **Luke 12:33**

PRAYER: Jesus, help me to live like You are the greatest reward. Thank You that what You have to offer is better than anything the world can offer me. Amen.

REFLECTION/APPLICATION: What is the difference between what the world promises and what Jesus promises? How have you personally experienced or seen someone else experience the world's deception in offering something that will never satisfy? How do our lives reflect what we value most and what does your life currently reflect that you value most?

UNASHAMED

For I am not ashamed of the gospel, because it is the power
of God that brings salvation to everyone who believes: first
to the Jew, then to the Gentile.

Romans 1:16

> The world can't afford for God's people to live ashamed
> of the gospel. Share it and live it boldly and unashamed.

YOU AND I HAVE TWO OPTIONS: to live wholeheartedly for Jesus or to do our own thing and then look back wishing that we had lived for Him. We have an opportunity every day to live for what is fleeting or for what is eternal. Either we can let the light of Jesus shine bright within us or we can allow fear to convince us to keep it hidden.

I challenge you to live for eternity for two reasons: (1) Jesus is worthy, and (2) the world needs Him.

It's not a matter of if every knee will bow and every tongue confess that Jesus is Lord, it's a matter of when. The gift of salvation is for everyone who receives it, but people won't know if they aren't told. The responsibility to share the gospel falls on not just a select group of believers but all who follow Jesus. You are called and equipped to share the Good News and live the truth of God's Word boldly.

You weren't given the Light of the World to keep the hope of who He is to yourself. You weren't given the truth and instruction of His Word to live according to the world's standard. The world around you is more desperate for a Savior with every moment that passes. People who don't know Jesus can't afford for those of us who do know Him to live ashamed or held back by fear of human opinion. He is the answer, and He lives within you.

People will reject you, but they rejected Him first. Don't allow the fear of rejection to stop you from seeing people receive the gift of who Jesus is because of the life that you live. There is no greater gift, other than knowing Him, than introducing someone to God and seeing their life transformed by His love.

Know His Word and live His Word. What you say is important, but how you live should confirm what you say. When people recognize His love in you, point them in His direction. Tell the story of how He transformed your life.

Let your life be evidence of a living God. You have no reason to be ashamed of the hope you have and every reason to be proud to live for His name's sake.

> Let your life be evidence
> of a living God.

If anyone is ashamed of me and my words in this adulterous and sinful generation, the Son of Man will be ashamed
of them when he comes in his Father's glory with the holy
angels.

Mark 8:38

PRAYER: Jesus, help me to live unashamed for You so
that the world around me comes to know You. I want to
be known for the boldness of my faith in You. Amen.

REFLECTION/APPLICATION: What hinders you from
living unashamed of the gospel? How does today's devotion encourage you to be bolder in sharing and living
God's Word?

A WAY IN THE WILDERNESS

See, I am doing a new thing!
    Now it springs up; do you not perceive it?
I am making a way in the wilderness
    and streams in the wasteland.

Isaiah 43:19

> The impossible in your life is simply an opportunity for God to reveal who He is and His ability to do what only He can do.

A MIRACLE-WORKING GOD cannot be limited by what appears impossible. The One the mountains and seas obey can make a way where there appears to be no way. When He does what only He can do, it is undeniable evidence of who He is. It opens eyes to the truth of His Word. The impossible doesn't intimidate God; it provides Him with an opportunity to reveal His power. When He intervenes, things change. When He is involved, nothing is impossible.

He walks on water.

The raging sea calms in an instant at the sound of His voice.

Streams flow through the desert on His authority.

Seas split when He commands them to.

Blind eyes are opened.

Deaf ears hear.

The lame walk.

Demons flee.

Captives are free.

The dead rise.

And death is defeated.

Why would we yield to the impossible instead of an all-powerful, miracle-working God who is still at work today? What is it that you need Him to do for you? His power lives on the inside of His people. He has given us mountain-moving, impossible-defeating authority. Your seemingly impossible circumstance is no exception. He is still breathing life into dead things. He is still restoring what seems lost. He is still making rivers through deserts and highways through oceans. Our lack of belief doesn't

A miracle-working God cannot be limited by what appears impossible.

change the reality of who He is, but it hinders us and others from experiencing the magnitude of His power.

Don't allow doubt to rob you from living in the abundance of believing that He is who He says He is and will do what He says He will do. Invite Him to invade what appears impossible in your life and the lives of those around you and watch Him do what only He can do. Activate the authority He has given to you. Expect Him to make a way. Allow Him to put His glory on display through the seemingly hopeless situations in your life so that others might come to know Him because of your belief in His power.

Seasons change, but He remains the same. The God who makes a way is still moving mountains today. There is nothing He cannot do, and there is no one He cannot redeem.

There is nothing too hard for God.

> Jesus looked at them and said, "With man this is impossible, but with God all things are possible."
>
> **Matthew 19:26**

PRAYER: Jesus, help me to live like I believe that nothing is impossible for You. Thank You that You make a way where there is no way. Amen.

REFLECTION/APPLICATION: Which of the miracles Jesus performed when He walked the earth is your favorite to read about? Why do you struggle or think others struggle with believing that God is still doing the impossible today? What impossible situation are you believing for Him to turn around?

DAY 50

WONDERFULLY MADE

For you created my inmost being;
　　you knit me together in my mother's womb.
I praise you because I am fearfully and wonderfully
　　made;
　　your works are wonderful,
I know that full well.

Psalm 139:13–14

> You are the wonderful work of God on display! Praise Him for the beautiful and unique way He created you.

THE TRUTH OF GOD'S WORD is powerful enough to break chains of comparison, insecurity, and purposeless- ness off your life. I've often wrestled throughout my life with feeling too ordinary or insignificant to be used by God. When I recognized that His ability to use me has nothing to do with

> He uses what appears ordinary to
> reveal His glory in undeniable ways.

who I am and everything to do with who He is, that changed everything. I remember Him once whispering these words to my heart, "I am perfect in all of My ways. I am intentional in all that I do. You and the way I created you are no exception to these truths about who I am."

If you consider your Creator and the work of His hands, you really can't hold on to the belief that you are ordinary and insignificant or that He made any mistakes when He made you. He is intentional in all that He does, and He is perfect in His design. It's not in His nature to create purposeless things.

He uses what appears ordinary to reveal His glory in undeniable ways.

He sees things so much differently than we do.

A moment spent criticizing or comparing the way He created you is a moment wasted. Don't live held back by the lie of insignificance any longer. He wouldn't have created you if He didn't have a perfect plan for your life to advance His kingdom. Uniqueness is the beauty of His design. If we were all created the same way with the same gifts, little would be accomplished, and life would be a lot less beautiful.

Don't be sorry about the way your Maker made you, because He surely isn't, and it's His opinion that matters. Thank Him for the way He created you, even the things you most wish He would have done differently. It will transform the way you see yourself and even the way you celebrate others.

He delights in you. Walk freely in who He has called you to be, and do what He has called you to do.

> Those who look to him are radiant;
>   their faces are never covered with shame.
> **Psalm 34:5**

PRAYER: Jesus, help me to see myself and others the way You do. Thank You for the promise that You are intentional in all that You do and design. Amen.

REFLECTION/APPLICATION: Write down a list of things you want to celebrate about the way God created you. How does who you are reveal the evidence of who He is?

THE BEST IS YET TO COME

For I consider that the sufferings of this present time are not worth comparing with the glory that is to be revealed to us.

Romans 8:18 ESV

Suffering is an unavoidable part of your life, but it will never compare to the joy that's coming!

YOU CAN FIX YOUR HEART either on the pain of suffering or on the promise of glory, which will be revealed to you through Jesus. You can either live in turmoil, constantly overwhelmed by the unknown, or you can live in the blessed assurance of what is to come.

We will all experience suffering, but suffering is not the end of the story for those who trust and follow Jesus. We are living for a bigger picture and an eternal promise we can cling to despite anything we face in this present moment.

> When you don't have the answers, He does. When you can't carry the weight of it all, He can.

There is joy and peace for today and bright hope for tomorrow because of the assurance we have in Jesus. We can live continually in confident anticipation because every word He speaks is true and every promise He has made will be fulfilled. There will be hard days and hard moments, even hard months and hard years. Things won't always make sense. Things will take place that we don't understand and cause us to feel defeated, but we will not be destroyed.

When you feel crushed by the suffering you see all around you or are personally facing, take heart—there is nothing unknown or unseen by God. He is faithful, sovereign, and in control when things feel out of control and painful. When you don't have the answers, He does. When you can't carry the weight of it all, He can.

We have all that we need to keep moving forward in trust today. He is no stranger to our suffering. He can sympathize with it and has given His Word as a guide to navigate it on this side of heaven. You may not know how long this trial will last, but you can trust that He will see you through it. You can rest in the unfailing promise of who He is. You may never see the full picture on this side of heaven, but there will be a day with no more tears. In and through Him, the BEST is yet to come.

> However, as it is written:
>
> "What no eye has seen,
>   what no ear has heard,
> and what no human mind has conceived"—
>   the things God has prepared for those who love him.
>
>   **1 Corinthians 2:9**

PRAYER: Jesus, help me to hope in You. You are in the midst of the trials I face. Thank You for being constant and in control. Amen.

REFLECTION/APPLICATION: How does the promise of what's to come help you respond to present hardship? What does it mean to you that Jesus is not a stranger to your suffering?

DAY 52

THE STRENGTH OF YOUR HEART

My flesh and my heart may fail,
but God is the strength of my heart
and my portion forever.

Psalm 73:26

God is constant and unchanging. No matter who and what comes and goes, He remains the same, and He is all that you need.

I'VE NEVER HAD a great relationship with change, especially unexpected change. I like to know what is coming when it's coming and to have the opportunity to plan accordingly. Can anyone relate? I've learned, though, that life generally doesn't work that way. More often than not, we have a plan, but things don't go according to that plan.

Psalm 73:26 has always been one of my favorite Scriptures. It reminds me of the One who remains constant and unfailing, no matter what changes or fails in my life. It reminds me of my desperate need for Jesus and keeps me running back to Him when I face the unexpected or when life feels out of control.

It's not a matter of if your heart and flesh will fail but when they will fail.

It's not a matter of if people will fail you but when they will fail you.

It's not a matter of if things will change throughout your life but when they will change.

Not just once, but many times, sometimes multiple times in the same day.

When your heart fails, He remains constant and unfailing.

When your flesh fails, He remains constant and unfailing.

When people fail you, He remains constant and unfailing.

Your heart, feelings, thoughts, and emotions will deceive you, but He never will.

Nothing will change who He is. He is in control.

The unchanging promise of who Jesus is, is your strength and the hope you have to hold fast to all the days of your life.

He is a strong tower, a place of rest and refuge. He strengthens you to carry on in the face of weakness, weariness, exhaustion, and confusion.

> When your flesh fails,
> He remains constant and unfailing.

He is your portion, your lot in life, the greatest treasure you will ever have. Don't lean on your own strength or understanding today. Both will let you down. Lean and depend on the One who is constant and unfailing, whose strength never runs out. No matter what you lack or lose, you still have everything you need in Jesus.

He is constant, He is good, and He is kind.

> The name of the Lord is a strong tower;
>   the righteous man runs into it and is safe.
> **Proverbs 18:10 ESV**

PRAYER: Jesus, grow me in confidence of Your unchanging goodness. Thank You for being the One I can run to when my heart and flesh fail. Amen.

REFLECTION/APPLICATION: How have your heart and flesh proven unreliable? How does the unfailing promise of who Jesus is change the way you view or experience change and the unexpected?

DAY 53

SPIRIT + TRUTH

But the hour is coming, and is now here, when the true worshipers will worship the Father in spirit and truth, for the Father is seeking such people to worship him.

John 4:23 ESV

Live a lifestyle of worship. Bring your sincere heart before God, not a performance. Your honesty moves His heart.

WORSHIP IS MORE than a Sunday morning experience; it is our continual response to who God is. Worship is a lifestyle, not a show to be put on once or twice a week. The Father is seeking those who are living for Him, not just those who say the right things or play the part in certain settings. He is looking for those who worship Him sincerely in the seen and unseen places.

Don't get me wrong, it's so important that we come together as the body of Christ, but the way we live our lives outside the

> When it comes to worship,
> Jesus is after your heart,
> not a performance.

walls of a church building is the true test of whether or not we are truly living for Him. Our gifts are meant to be used for His glory, not for our own gain. We may be able to fake it or fool each other, but we can't fool Him. People look at the outward appearance, but He looks at the heart—and He sees it all.

When He looks at your heart, will He see Himself seated on the throne?

When He looks at your life, will He see Himself at the center?

When it comes to worship, Jesus is after your heart, not a performance.

When it comes to worship, Jesus is more concerned with your heart posture than your appearance.

When it comes to worship, Jesus is more concerned with your sincerity than your talents or giftings.

When it comes to worship, He is worthy of more than a song.

When it comes to worship, how you live should reflect what you say.

Don't just sing Him a song; give Him your everything.

Don't idolize the lesser thing. Make Jesus the main thing. Worship Him in spirit and truth. He died for you, so when it comes to your life, He is worthy of it all.

> Therefore, since we are receiving a kingdom that cannot be
> shaken, let us be thankful, and so worship God acceptably
> with reverence and awe, for our "God is a consuming fire."
> **Hebrews 12:28-29**

PRAYER: Jesus, help me to live a lifestyle of worship.
You died for me so I will live wholeheartedly for You.
Amen.

REFLECTION/APPLICATION: What hinders you from
living a lifestyle of worship? When Jesus looks at your
heart, what do you desire for Him to see? How does that
desire shape the way you worship?

DAY 54

MADE NEW

Therefore, if anyone is in Christ, he is a new creation. The old has passed away; behold, the new has come.

2 Corinthians 5:17 ESV

Jesus doesn't just make you better, He makes you new.

THE WORLD AND THINGS of it should be charged with identity theft. When sin entered God's perfect plan, humanity's identity as God's perfect creation, made in His image and for His glory, was manipulated into something it was never meant to be. You and I live daily in the consequence of sin entering in. Our pain, insecurity, and confusion about who we are and whose we are were never God's intention or design; it is simply a result of humankind's disobedience to His plan.

But there is good news! Hope is not lost. A Savior came to save us, set us free, remind us of who we are because of whose we are, and take back what sin has stolen. There is hope in Him.

When Jesus hung on the cross, He had you in mind.

Entering into a relationship with Jesus doesn't just make you a better person, it makes you a new creation. Knowing Him doesn't just change who you are, it transforms who you are from the inside out. When you surrender your life to Jesus and submit to the truth of His Word, you become who you were always made to be.

You are no longer defined by who you are and what you have done, but who He is and what He's done perfectly. I get it, it's hard to comprehend, especially when we feel so undeserving of His grace and love. Don't live entangled by your past because you are unwilling to receive what He has freely given.

When Jesus hung on the cross, He had you in mind. The joy set before Him was you and your redemption. Live in the promise of newness in Christ. There is nothing and no one He cannot redeem.

Don't exhaust yourself by trying harder. Receive the gift of salvation and walk in continual relationship with your Savior. The more time you spend with Him, the more like Him you will become. It's time to let go of what has hindered you and step forward in freedom.

I have been crucified with Christ and I no longer live, but Christ lives in me. The life I now live in the body, I live by faith in the Son of God, who loved me and gave himself for me.

Galatians 2:20

PRAYER: Jesus, help me to leave the past behind and live as the new creation You have called me to be. Thank You for not just making me better but making me new. Amen.

REFLECTION/APPLICATION: What defined you before Jesus made you new? What defines you now as a new creation in Him?

DAY 55

FREE INDEED

So if the Son sets you free, you will be free indeed.

John 8:36

> Those God sets free are completely free! Walk in the
> fullness of freedom you have found in Jesus.

THERE IS AN INTENTIONAL PURPOSE for the word *indeed* in this passage. It doesn't just say "who the Son sets free is free." The reality of our freedom is intentionally emphasized through the declaration of the word *indeed*. If you have given your life to Christ, you are free indeed.

When He hung on the cross, you were on His mind. When He declared "it is finished" and died, the price for your freedom was bought with His life. Then, He rose, just as He promised, proving His victory over death. In His victory, your victory is found. To Him, the price of your freedom was worth the cost of His life.

Every day, you have a choice to live in freedom or to return to what once enslaved you. No one can make the choice for you,

> Every day, you have a choice
> to live in freedom or to return
> to what once enslaved you.

but His Word invites and empowers you to choose freedom. Choose to live the full and free life Jesus died so that you could have. He paid the ultimate price so that you could have life and life abundant. He didn't die for you to continue living bound by sin and shame. I can only imagine how it breaks His heart when those He came to set free continue to live like they are bound.

Your freedom is the reward of His suffering. Your life is evidence of His amazing love. You don't have to earn your freedom; you just have to accept the work of the cross and live out the result. You simply have to live like His Word is true.

One of the most beautiful things about true freedom in Christ is that it's contagious. When you live free indeed, others can't help but recognize it, and many will desire that freedom themselves. Your choice to walk in freedom will lead those around you to freedom from bondage as well. It's inevitable.

Other than knowing Jesus, there is no greater joy in this life than watching others experience the freedom you have found in Him. Who the Son sets free is free indeed! Don't take for granted the gift of receiving the reward of His sacrifice. In Him, there is so much more.

> Therefore, there is now no condemnation for those who are in Christ Jesus, because through Christ Jesus the law of the Spirit who gives life has set you free from the law of sin and death.
>
> **Romans 8:1–2**

PRAYER: Jesus, help me to live a life of contagious freedom found in You alone. Thank You that You died so that I could live an abundant life. Amen.

REFLECTION/APPLICATION: What is something you were once enslaved to that you often find yourself tempted to return to? How does the fact that Jesus had you in mind when He hung on the cross challenge you to walk in freedom from that temptation?

WALK
IN THE SPIRIT

So I say, let the Holy Spirit guide your lives. Then you won't
be doing what your sinful nature craves.

Galatians 5:16 NLT

God has given us the gift of the Holy Spirit as our Helper.
Allow Him to guide your life as you live in this world but
not of it.

COULDN'T COMPLETE this book without emphasizing
the importance of the power of the Holy Spirit in your life.
I find that He has often been misrepresented, but that doesn't
change His vitality and the reality of who He is.

The best gift God has given us is the gift of Himself—Father,
Son, and Spirit. Every part of who He is, is of equal importance
to our lives as believers. You can't have one without the other.

When you ask Him to come into your heart, He doesn't just give a portion of Himself; you receive the fullness of who He is.

When Jesus ascended to heaven, He actually told the disciples that it was better that He would go because of the One who the Father was sending in His place. Since Jesus couldn't physically be everywhere at once, God sent His Spirit to dwell within us so that His presence would be with us wherever we go.

> But I tell you the truth, it is to your advantage that I go away; for if I do not go away, the Helper (Comforter, Advocate, Intercessor—Counselor, Strengthener, Standby) will not come to you; but if I go, I will send Him (the Holy Spirit) to you [to be in close fellowship with you].
>
> **John 16:7 AMP**

The Spirit is a Helper, Comforter, and Guide.

One of the greatest mistakes we could ever make is to undervalue the gift of God's Spirit due to misconception or misunderstanding who He is. If you are in Christ, you are in the world but not of it. You are held to a different standard. Without the guidance of the Holy Spirit and His power at work within you, it would be impossible to live a life that is pleasing to God. The Spirit protects us from the temptation of the world by empowering us to live according to the standard of God's Word.

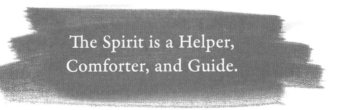

The Spirit is a Helper, Comforter, and Guide.

Walk in the Spirit. Allow His power to be the reigning authority in your life. Rest in the awareness of His presence that is with
you always.

> But the Helper, the Holy Spirit, whom the Father will send
> in my name, he will teach you all things and bring to your
> remembrance all that I have said to you.
>
> **John 14:26 ESV**

PRAYER: Jesus, thank You for the fullness of who You
are. Help me to live led by the Spirit according to the
standard of Your Word. Amen.

REFLECTION/APPLICATION: How have you experienced the help, comfort, and guidance of the Holy Spirit?
How do His presence and power protect you from living
according to your fleshly desires?

DAY 57

CLOSER

Come close to God, and God will come close to you. Wash
your hands, you sinners; purify your hearts, for your loyalty
is divided between God and the world.

James 4:8 NLT

The closer you get to the heart of God, the further away
the cares of the world will become. Draw near to Him
and He will draw near to you.

JESUS WAS THE ONLY ANSWER to reconciliation between humanity and God where sin once separated us from
the ability to walk in relationship with Him. The reward of His
sacrifice is a relationship with Him. He hung on the cross because
He couldn't bear the thought of being eternally separated from
you. He loves you so much that He gave His life in order to restore
what sin destroyed.

To Him, you were (and are) worth it.

You were created for a relationship with God. Relationships
don't grow on their own; they require intentionality. Your relation-

> The closer you are to Jesus,
> the further away the cares
> of the world will seem.

ship with Jesus isn't an exception. Growing in relationship with Jesus will require your intentional pursuit. His instruction is to draw near to Him, and His promise is that He will draw near to you.

You will never arrive at a point in your life when He doesn't desire to draw you closer or to take you deeper. He wants you to know Him more every day, because the more you know Him, the more you will trust His character and live a life of surrender to Him.

Surrender to Him is where true freedom and abundance are found.

Jesus invites you to dwell in Him, to abide in Him. He wants you to walk with Him, talk with Him, and confidently trust in His Word. He calls you to give Him your wholehearted devotion because you can't have both Him and the world. The two will always be at war with each other for your heart's attention.

Give the attention of your heart to the One who died for you. He is the only One who will satisfy.

The closer you are to Jesus, the further away the cares of the world will seem. The closer you are to Jesus, the more you will realize that He is what is worthwhile in this one life on earth you have to live. He deserves so much more than a divided heart. He deserves everything.

There is nothing better than knowing Jesus.
There is no love like His love for you.
Draw near to Him and He will draw near to you.

> Let us draw near to God with a sincere heart and with the
> full assurance that faith brings, having our hearts sprinkled to
> cleanse us from a guilty conscience and having our bodies
> washed with pure water.
>
> **Hebrews 10:22**

PRAYER: Jesus, help me to live wholeheartedly for You.
Thank You for drawing near to me when I draw near to
You. Amen.

REFLECTION/APPLICATION: What does it mean for
your loyalty to be divided between God and the world?
What do you need to "wash your hands clean of" in
order to draw closer to Jesus?

THE POTTER
+ THE CLAY

But now, O Lord, you are our Father;
we are the clay, and you are our potter;
we are all the work of your hand.

Isaiah 64:8 ESV

Allow yourself to be molded like clay in God's hands.
He will create something more beautiful out of your life
than you could ever imagine.

HE IS THE POTTER; we are the clay.

We are the canvas; He is the painter.

In order to be made into a useful creation, clay has to be placed into a potter's hand, thrown on their wheel, and then put through the fire. It has to be formed, molded and shaped, and refined. Clay can be made into many different things, but no matter how it's shaped, every step is necessary in order for it to fulfill its intended purpose. When the clay is molded into a masterpiece, it simply serves the purpose for which its Maker created it.

This process can be compared to our spiritual lives.

Being made into who God has created us to be is a lifelong process. Similar to clay, we are each made with a uniquely designed purpose, though we all started as dust. In order to become something useful, we have to be placed in Jesus's hand, yield to His process, and be put through the fire to be formed, molded and shaped, and refined to reflect His image more clearly. Again, every step is necessary in order to fulfill the purpose for which He created us. He creates us and when we place our lives into His hands, we are molded into a vessel that reveals His glory.

Our willingness to allow Him to shape us will determine how useful we are. We decide whether or not we will put our lives on the Potter's wheel and allow Him to make of us whatever He sees fit to be useful for kingdom purposes.

So often we want to skip a step and run from the refining. We wish Jesus would hurry up and finish the work He has started in and through us. Many of us have a preference as to what we would like to become. We think we know best, and we want to be seen as better than the rest. God isn't in a hurry like we are, and He won't yield to our preference, for He knows exactly who He designed us to be and how He wants to use us.

> He will make you a vessel
> more beautiful than you ever
> could have imagined.

Place your life in the Potter's hands, and He will make you a vessel more beautiful than you ever could have imagined. As you are continually molded, don't compare your purpose to the purpose of the vessels around you. Serve the purpose for which the Master created you to reveal His glory with joy.

You are defined by your Maker.

> For we are God's handiwork, created in Christ Jesus to do good works, which God prepared in advance for us to do.
>
> **Ephesians 2:10**

PRAYER: Jesus, I want to be continually shaped into who You have created me to be. Help me to be like moldable clay in Your hands. Amen.

REFLECTION/APPLICATION: How would you describe the current season of becoming that you are in? What does the analogy of the potter and the clay reveal about the importance of the process?

DAY 59

SURRENDER IS SUCCESS

Study this Book of Instruction continually. Meditate on it day and night so you will be sure to obey everything written in it. Only then will you prosper and succeed in all you do.

Joshua 1:8 NLT

> The true key to success is living in obedience to God's Word. Be in His Word continually so you know what you have been called to do.

EVERY ONE OF US has a desire to live a life that leaves an impact. We all desire success in some way, shape, or form. You and I live in a culture that is consumed by the pursuit of earthly success. We are surrounded by people striving for fame, power, wealth, health, and countless other things. We're constantly being bombarded with an empty promise that we can find security and satisfaction in what the world has to offer. The

> # In His kingdom,
> # the key to success is submission
> # to His instruction.

world's standard of success is for us to build our own kingdom or even to idolize someone else's.

God has a different standard when it comes to success. In His kingdom, the key to success is submission to His instruction. Success, according to God's standard, is for His will to be done on earth as it is in heaven. It doesn't mean we can't have things, but it does mean we have to recognize that in Him alone, we have everything we need. We have to be willing to hold everything else with a loose grip.

The world says that the more you have, the more successful you are. The Word says if you have Jesus, you have everything you need.

The world says the more people who know you, the more successful you are. The Word says your life is about leading others to know Jesus.

The world says the more you strive, the more successful you will be. The Word challenges you to live a life of surrender that leads to abundant life.

Every day, you have a choice to make. Will you live according to an earthly standard of success or an eternal one? Will you live a life in pursuit of what is quickly fleeting or in pursuit of a kingdom that lasts forever?

God's Word promises that if you live in submission to His instruction, you will be successful in all that you do because He will be glorified. No promises He speaks are empty. Instead of striving for fleeting success, live in submission to God's Word and leave an eternal impact.

> If you fully obey the LORD your God and carefully follow all his commands I give you today, the LORD your God will set you high above all the nations on earth.
>
> **Deuteronomy 28:1**

PRAYER: Jesus, help me to live in pursuit of Your standard of success. Amen.

REFLECTION/APPLICATION: Where have you tried to find success or security that has ultimately led to disappointment? What is the difference between submission to God's Word and striving?

THE GOD WHO GOES BEFORE YOU

The LORD himself goes before you and will be with you; he will never leave you nor forsake you. Do not be afraid; do not be discouraged.

Deuteronomy 31:8

Wherever you go and whatever you do, God goes before you. You have nothing to fear for He is with you.

SECURITY ISN'T FOUND in where you are going or what you are doing but in whom you are walking with. As this 60-day journey comes to an end, I challenge you to continue walking with Jesus. You need to know that you are never alone in the days ahead. You never have been, and you never will be. The One who walks with you also goes before you, remains behind you, and surrounds you on every side. He has gone before you, no matter where you go or what you do.

> The One who holds it all together
> holds your life in His hands.

You will face many unknowns in the days ahead, but the Good Shepherd is leading you. He is your Father, your Savior, your Helper, your Guide, your Comfort, your Protector, your Redeemer, and your closest and most unfailing friend.

The One who called you according to His purpose and who calls you His own is also leading you every surrendered step of the way. He will be faithful to complete the work He has started or continued in you over the last sixty days if you continue to trust and follow the sound of His voice and hold fast to the truth of His Word. Nothing will ever compare to the abundance you will find in submitting your life to His authority.

The One who holds it all together holds your life in His hands.

Not only can He be trusted with your yes, but He will do more with it than you ever could have hoped, imagined, or dreamed. It makes no sense, but we learn by living that freedom is found in letting go of what we want in order to gain the fullness of what He has prepared for us. No one knows what's best for you like the One who knows you best.

Know Him.

Trust Him.

Follow Him.

Know His Word.

Live His Word.

Teach and share His Word.

May your life be undeniable evidence to a hurting world of the hope of Jesus.

If you are able to point just one person in His direction, it's all worth it. I'll end with the passage we started with.

> Trust in the LORD with all your heart
>   and lean not on your own understanding;
> in all your ways submit to him,
>   and he will make your paths straight.
>
> **Proverbs 3:5–6**

PRAYER: Jesus, thank You that there is nowhere I go that You don't go before me. Help me to live a life that reveals the undeniable evidence of who You are to the world around me. Amen.

REFLECTION/APPLICATION: How does the promise that God goes before you increase your confidence to walk in surrender? How have you grown in your knowledge of, trust in, and desire to follow Jesus in the last sixty days?

CLOSING PRAYER

Jesus, I won't just know of You; I will know You personally. I won't just know You; I will trust and follow You, wherever You lead me and whatever it costs me. I will live a lifestyle of obedience, and I will experience the abundance You promise to those who take You at your word as a result. Amen.

SALVATION PRAYER

Jesus, I recognize that I have sinned and fallen short of Your standard, and I ask You to forgive me. I believe that You are the Son of God, that You died to pay the price for the sins that I could never repay, and that You rose again three days later. I invite You into my heart and surrender my life to You from this day forward. Thank You for the gift of grace and the guidance of Your Spirit. Help me to know, trust, and follow You. Amen.

SCRIPTURE REFERENCE GUIDE

Trust in the Lord with all your heart
and lean not on your own understanding;
in all your ways submit to him,
and he will make your paths straight.
Proverbs 3:5-6

We know that we have come to know him if we keep his commands.
1 John 2:3

Remain in me, as I also remain in you. No branch can bear fruit by itself; it must remain in the vine. Neither can you bear fruit unless you remain in me.

John 15:4

Blessed is the one
who does not walk in step with the wicked
or stand in the way that sinners take
or sit in the company of mockers,

but whose delight is in the law of the Lord,
and who meditates on his law day and night.
That person is like a tree planted by streams of water,
which yields its fruit in season
and whose leaf does not wither—
whatever they do prospers.

Psalm 1:1–3

For God has not given us a spirit of fear, but of power and of love and of a sound mind.

2 Timothy 1:7 NKJV

And the peace of God, which surpasses all understanding, will guard your hearts and your minds in Christ Jesus.

Philippians 4:7 ESV

For God so loved the world, that he gave his only Son, that whoever believes in him should not perish but have eternal life.

John 3:16 ESV

Your unfailing love is better than life itself;
how I praise you!

Psalm 63:3 NLT

And I pray that you, being rooted and established in love, may have power, together with all the Lord's holy people, to grasp how wide and long and high and deep is the love of Christ, and to know this love that surpasses knowledge—that you may be filled to the measure of all the fullness of God.

Ephesians 3:17–19

If you love me, keep my commands.

John 14:15

Do not merely listen to the word, and so deceive yourselves. Do what it says. Anyone who listens to the word but does not do what it says is like someone who looks at his face in a mirror and, after looking at himself, goes away and immediately forgets what he looks like. But whoever looks intently into the perfect law that gives freedom, and continues in it—not forgetting what they have heard, but doing it—they will be blessed in what they do.

James 1:22–25

Therefore everyone who hears these words of mine and puts them into practice is like a wise man who built his house on the rock. The rain came down, the streams rose, and the winds blew and beat against that house; yet it did not fall, because it had its foundation on the rock. But everyone who hears these words of mine and does not put them into practice is like a foolish man who built his house on sand. The rain came down, the streams rose, and the winds blew and beat against that house, and it fell with a great crash.

Matthew 7:24–27

Jesus Christ is the same yesterday and today and forever.
Hebrews 13:8

You will seek me and find me when you seek me with all your heart.
Jeremiah 29:13

So I say to you: Ask and it will be given to you; seek and you will find; knock and the door will be opened to you. For everyone who asks receives; the one who seeks finds; and to the one who knocks, the door will be opened.

Luke 11:9–10

"Though the mountains be shaken
   and the hills be removed,

yet my unfailing love for you will not be shaken
    nor my covenant of peace be removed,"
  says the Lord, who has compassion on you.
                              Isaiah 54:10

Where can I go from your Spirit?
  Where can I flee from your presence?
If I go up to the heavens, you are there;
  if I make my bed in the depths, you are there.
If I rise on the wings of the dawn,
  if I settle on the far side of the sea,
even there your hand will guide me,
  your right hand will hold me fast.
                          Psalm 139:7–10

But you are not like that, for you are a chosen people. You are royal priests, a holy nation, God's very own possession. As a result, you can show others the goodness of God, for he called you out of the darkness into his wonderful light.

                              1 Peter 2:9 NLT

Do not love the world or anything in the world. If anyone loves the world, love for the Father is not in them. For everything in the world—the lust of the flesh, the lust of the eyes, and the pride of life—comes not from the Father but from the world. The world and its desires pass away, but whoever does the will of God lives forever.

                              1 John 2:15–17

For the grace of God has appeared that offers salvation to all people. It teaches us to say "No" to ungodliness and worldly passions, and to live self-controlled, upright and godly lives in this present age, while

we wait for the blessed hope—the appearing of the glory of our great
God and Savior, Jesus Christ, who gave himself for us to redeem us from
all wickedness and to purify for himself a people that are his very own,
eager to do what is good.

Titus 2:11–14

For it is by grace you have been saved, through faith—and this is not
from yourselves, it is the gift of God— not by works, so that no one can
boast.

Ephesians 2:8–9

Out of his fullness we have all received grace in place of grace already
given.

John 1:16

> The LORD directs the steps of the godly.
> He delights in every detail of their lives.
> Though they stumble, they will never fall,
> for the LORD holds them by the hand.
> **Psalm 37:23–24 NLT**

> Because you are precious in my eyes,
> and honored, and I love you,
> I give men in return for you,
> peoples in exchange for your life.
> **Isaiah 43:4 ESV**

For you are a people holy to the LORD your God, and the LORD has chosen
you to be a people for his treasured possession, out of all the peoples
who are on the face of the earth.

Deuteronomy 14:2 ESV

What is the price of two sparrows—one copper coin? But not a single sparrow can fall to the ground without your Father knowing it. And the very hairs on your head are all numbered. So don't be afraid; you are more valuable to God than a whole flock of sparrows.

Matthew 10:29–31 NLT

Your kingdom is an everlasting kingdom,
and your dominion endures through all generations.

The LORD is trustworthy in all he promises
and faithful in all he does.

Psalm 145:13

For no matter how many promises God has made, they are "Yes" in Christ. And so through him the "Amen" is spoken by us to the glory of God.

2 Corinthians 1:20

But seek first his kingdom and his righteousness, and all these things will be given to you as well.

Matthew 6:33

I am the true vine, and my Father is the gardener. He cuts off every branch in me that bears no fruit, while every branch that does bear fruit he prunes so that it will be even more fruitful. You are already clean because of the word I have spoken to you. Remain in me, as I also remain in you. No branch can bear fruit by itself; it must remain in the vine. Neither can you bear fruit unless you remain in me.

I am the vine; you are the branches. If you remain in me and I in you, you will bear much fruit; apart from me you can do nothing. If you do not remain in me, you are like a branch that is thrown away and withers; such branches are picked up, thrown into the fire and burned. If you remain in me and my words remain in you, ask whatever you wish, and it will be done for you. This is to my Father's glory, that you bear much fruit, showing yourselves to be my disciples.

John 15:1-8

Jesus replied: "'Love the Lord your God with all your heart and with all your soul and with all your mind.' This is the first and greatest commandment."

Matthew 22:37-38

"For my thoughts are not your thoughts,
neither are your ways my ways,"
declares the Lord.
"As the heavens are higher than the earth,
so are my ways higher than your ways
and my thoughts than your thoughts."
Isaiah 55:8-9

I have seen the burden God has laid on the human race. He has made everything beautiful in its time. He has also set eternity in the human heart; yet no one can fathom what God has done from beginning to end.

Ecclesiastes 3:10-11

Now faith is the substance of things hoped for, the evidence of things not seen.

Hebrews 11:1 NKJV

He replied, "Because you have so little faith. Truly I tell you, if you have faith as small as a mustard seed, you can say to this mountain, 'Move from here to there,' and it will move. Nothing will be impossible for you."

Matthew 17:20

As Jesus was walking beside the Sea of Galilee, he saw two brothers, Simon called Peter and his brother Andrew. They were casting a net into the lake, for they were fishermen. "Come, follow me," Jesus said, "and I will send you out to fish for people." At once they left their nets and followed him.

Matthew 4:18–20

To this you were called, because Christ suffered for you, leaving you an example, that you should follow in his steps.

1 Peter 2:21

Commit your work to the LORD,
    and your plans will be established.
Proverbs 16:3 ESV

Your word *is* a lamp to my feet
And a light to my path.
Psalm 119:105 NKJV

By his divine power, God has given us everything we need for living a godly life. We have received all of this by coming to know him, the one who called us to himself by means of his marvelous glory and excellence.

2 Peter 1:3 NLT

All Scripture is God-breathed and is useful for teaching, rebuking, correcting and training in righteousness, so that the servant of God may be thoroughly equipped for every good work.

2 Timothy 3:16–17

Patient endurance is what you need now, so that you will continue to do God's will. Then you will receive all that he has promised.

Hebrews 10:36 NLT

But as for you, be strong and do not give up, for your work will be rewarded.

2 Chronicles 15:7

You will keep in perfect *and* constant peace *the one* whose mind is steadfast [that is, committed and focused on You—in both inclination and character],

Because he trusts *and* takes refuge in You [with hope and confident expectation].

Isaiah 26:3 AMP

Now may the Lord of peace himself give you peace at all times and in every way. The Lord be with all of you.

2 Thessalonians 3:16

So get rid of all the filth and evil in your lives, and humbly accept the word God has planted in your hearts, for it has the power to save your souls.

But don't just listen to God's word. You must do what it says. Otherwise, you are only fooling yourselves.

James 1:21–22 NLT

You were running a good race. Who cut in on you to keep you from obeying the truth? That kind of persuasion does not come from the one who calls you. "A little yeast works through the whole batch of dough."

Galatians 5:7–9

For we speak as messengers approved by God to be entrusted with the Good News. Our purpose is to please God, not people. He alone examines the motives of our hearts.

1 Thessalonians 2:4 NLT

Many are the plans in a person's heart,
but it is the Lord's purpose that prevails.

Proverbs 19:21

He must become greater and greater, and I must become less and less.

John 3:30 NLT

Am I now trying to win the approval of human beings, or of God? Or am I trying to please people? If I were still trying to please people, I would not be a servant of Christ.

Galatians 1:10

In the beginning was the Word, and the Word was with God, and the Word was God. . . . The Word became flesh and made his dwelling among us. We have seen his glory, the glory of the one and only Son, who came from the Father, full of grace and truth.

John 1:1, 14

God is not human, that he should lie,
  not a human being, that he should change his mind.
Does he speak and then not act?
  Does he promise and not fulfill?

Numbers 23:19

Every word of God proves true.
  He is a shield to all who come to him for protection.

Proverbs 30:5 NLT

You make known to me the path of life;
  in your presence there is fullness of joy;
  at your right hand are pleasures forevermore.

Psalm 16:11 ESV

These things I have spoken to you, that my joy may be in you, and that your joy may be full.

John 15:11 ESV

Rejoice always, pray continually, give thanks in all circumstances; for this is God's will for you in Christ Jesus.

1 Thessalonians 5:16–18

Don't worry about anything; instead, pray about everything. Tell God what you need, and thank him for all he has done. Then you will experience God's peace, which exceeds anything we can understand. His peace will guard your hearts and minds as you live in Christ Jesus.
Philippians 4:6–7 NLT

Rejoice in hope, be patient in tribulation, be constant in prayer.
Romans 12:12 ESV

But blessed is the one who trusts in the LORD,
whose confidence is in him.
They will be like a tree planted by the water
that sends out its roots by the stream.
It does not fear when heat comes;
its leaves are always green.
It has no worries in a year of drought
and never fails to bear fruit.
Jeremiah 17:7–8

Surely the righteous will never be shaken;
they will be remembered forever.
They will have no fear of bad news;
their hearts are steadfast, trusting in the LORD.
Psalm 112:6–7

Trust in the LORD forever,
for the LORD, the LORD himself, is the Rock eternal.
Isaiah 26:4

For everyone who has been born of God overcomes the world. And this is the victory that has overcome the world—our faith.
1 John 5:4 ESV

L<small>ORD</small>, the God of our ancestors, are you not the God who is in heaven? You rule over all the kingdoms of the nations. Power and might are in your hand, and no one can withstand you.

2 Chronicles 20:6

> I will bring that group through the fire
> > and make them pure.
> I will refine them like silver
> > and purify them like gold.
> They will call on my name,
> > and I will answer them.
> I will say, "These are my people,"
> > and they will say, "The L<small>ORD</small> is our God."

Zechariah 13:9 NLT

> See, I have refined you, though not as silver;
> > I have tested you in the furnace of affliction.

Isaiah 48:10

For once you were full of darkness, but now you have light from the Lord. So live as people of light! For this light within you produces only what is good and right and true.

Ephesians 5:8–9 NLT

You are the salt of the earth. But if the salt loses its saltiness, how can it be made salty again? It is no longer good for anything, except to be thrown out and trampled underfoot.

Matthew 5:13

Yet you do not know [the least thing] about what may happen in your life tomorrow. [What is secure in your life?] You are *merely* a vapor [like

a puff of smoke or a wisp of steam from a cooking pot] that is visible for
a little while and then vanishes [into thin air].

James 4:14 AMP

Teach us to number our days,
that we may gain a heart of wisdom.

Psalm 90:12

I waited patiently for the Lord;
he inclined to me and heard my cry.
He drew me up from the pit of destruction,
out of the miry bog,
and set my feet upon a rock,
making my steps secure.

Psalm 40:1–2 ESV

But those who wait for the Lord [who expect, look for,
and hope in Him]
Will gain new strength *and* renew their power;
They will lift up their wings [and rise up close to God] like
eagles [rising toward the sun];
They will run and not become weary,
They will walk and not grow tired.

Isaiah 40:31 AMP

The Lord is my shepherd; I shall not want.
He makes me lie down in green pastures.
He leads me beside still waters.
He restores my soul.
He leads me in paths of righteousness
for his name's sake.

Even though I walk through the valley of the shadow
    of death,
    I will fear no evil,
for you are with me;
    your rod and your staff,
    they comfort me.

You prepare a table before me
    in the presence of my enemies;
you anoint my head with oil;
    my cup overflows.
Surely goodness and mercy shall follow me ·
    all the days of my life,
and I shall dwell in the house of the Lᴏʀᴅ
    forever.

Psalm 23 ESV

Come to me, all you who are weary and burdened, and I will give you rest. Take my yoke upon you and learn from me, for I am gentle and humble in heart, and you will find rest for your souls. For my yoke is easy and my burden is light.

Matthew 11:28–30

So, my dear brothers and sisters, be strong and immovable. Always work enthusiastically for the Lord, for you know that nothing you do for the Lord is ever useless.

1 Corinthians 15:58 NLT

Blessed is the one who perseveres under trial because, having stood the test, that person will receive the crown of life that the Lord has promised to those who love him.

James 1:12

Therefore, since we are surrounded by such a huge crowd of witnesses to the life of faith, let us strip off every weight that slows us down, especially the sin that so easily trips us up. And let us run with endurance the race God has set before us. We do this by keeping our eyes on Jesus, the champion who initiates and perfects our faith. Because of the joy awaiting him, he endured the cross, disregarding its shame. Now he is seated in the place of honor beside God's throne.

Hebrews 12:1–2 NLT

I keep my eyes always on the LORD.
With him at my right hand, I will not be shaken.
Psalm 16:8

Let us not become weary in doing good, for at the proper time we will reap a harvest if we do not give up.

Galatians 6:9

Therefore, since through God's mercy we have this ministry, we do not lose heart.

2 Corinthians 4:1

Now to him who is able to do far more abundantly than all that we ask or think, according to the power at work within us.

Ephesians 3:20 ESV

And we know that in all things God works for the good of those who love him, who have been called according to his purpose.

Romans 8:28

So whether you eat or drink or whatever you do, do it all for the glory of God.

1 Corinthians 10:31

Then God said, "Let us make mankind in our image, in our likeness, so that they may rule over the fish in the sea and the birds in the sky, over the livestock and all the wild animals, and over all the creatures that move along the ground."

Genesis 1:26

> So do not fear, for I am with you;
> do not be dismayed, for I am your God.
> I will strengthen you and help you;
> I will uphold you with my righteous right hand.
>
> **Isaiah 41:10**

> I sought the LORD, and he answered me;
> he delivered me from all my fears.
>
> **Psalm 34:4**

Sitting down, Jesus called the Twelve and said, "Anyone who wants to be first must be the very last, and the servant of all."

Mark 9:35

In your relationships with one another, have the same mindset as Christ Jesus:

> Who, being in very nature God,
> did not consider equality with God something to be
> used to his own advantage;
> rather, he made himself nothing
> by taking the very nature of a servant,
> being made in human likeness.
> And being found in appearance as a man,
> he humbled himself by becoming obedient to death—
> even death on a cross!
>
> **Philippians 2:5–8**

So God has given both his promise and his oath. These two things are unchangeable because it is impossible for God to lie. Therefore, we who have fled to him for refuge can have great confidence as we hold to the hope that lies before us. This hope is a strong and trustworthy anchor for our souls. It leads us through the curtain into God's inner sanctuary.

Hebrews 6:18–19 NLT

And hope does not put us to shame, because God's love has been poured out into our hearts through the Holy Spirit, who has been given to us.

Romans 5:5

Enter through the narrow gate. For wide is the gate and broad is the road that leads to destruction, and many enter through it. But small is the gate and narrow the road that leads to life, and only a few find it.

Matthew 7:13–14

Not everyone who says to me, "Lord, Lord," will enter the kingdom of heaven, but only the one who does the will of my Father who is in heaven. Many will say to me on that day, "Lord, Lord, did we not prophesy in your name and in your name drive out demons and in your name perform many miracles?" Then I will tell them plainly, "I never knew you. Away from me, you evildoers!"

Matthew 7:21–23

By this everyone will know that you are my disciples, if you love one another.

John 13:35

Love is patient, love is kind. It does not envy, it does not boast, it is not proud. It does not dishonor others, it is not self-seeking, it is not easily angered, it keeps no record of wrongs. Love does not delight in evil but rejoices with the truth. It always protects, always trusts, always hopes, always perseveres.

1 Corinthians 13:4–7

And now these three remain: faith, hope and love. But the greatest of these is love.

1 Corinthians 13:13

My command is this: Love each other as I have loved you. Greater love has no one than this: to lay down one's life for one's friends.

John 15:12–13

> For the Lord God is a sun and shield;
> the Lord bestows favor and honor.
> No good thing does he withhold
> from those who walk uprightly.

Psalm 84:11 ESV

If you, then, though you are evil, know how to give good gifts to your children, how much more will your Father in heaven give good gifts to those who ask him!

Matthew 7:11

Consider it pure joy, my brothers and sisters, whenever you face trials of many kinds, because you know that the testing of your faith produces perseverance. Let perseverance finish its work so that you may be mature and complete, not lacking anything.

James 1:2–4

And the God of all grace, who called you to his eternal glory in Christ, after you have suffered a little while, will himself restore you and make you strong, firm and steadfast.

1 Peter 5:10

"We have here only five loaves of bread and two fish," they answered. "Bring them here to me," he said. And he directed the people to sit down on the grass. Taking the five loaves and the two fish and looking up to heaven, he gave thanks and broke the loaves. Then he gave them to the disciples, and the disciples gave them to the people. They all ate and were satisfied, and the disciples picked up twelve basketfuls of broken pieces that were left over. The number of those who ate was about five thousand men, besides women and children.

Matthew 14:17–21

"Bring the whole tithe into the storehouse, that there may be food in my house. Test me in this," says the Lord Almighty, "and see if I will not throw open the floodgates of heaven and pour out so much blessing that there will not be room enough to store it."

Malachi 3:10

And what do you benefit if you gain the whole world but lose your own soul? Is anything worth more than your soul?

Matthew 16:26 NLT

Sell your possessions and give to the poor. Provide purses for yourselves that will not wear out, a treasure in heaven that will never fail, where no thief comes near and no moth destroys.

Luke 12:33

For I am not ashamed of the gospel, because it is the power of God that brings salvation to everyone who believes: first to the Jew, then to the Gentile.

Romans 1:16

If anyone is ashamed of me and my words in this adulterous and sinful generation, the Son of Man will be ashamed of them when he comes in his Father's glory with the holy angels.

Mark 8:38

See, I am doing a new thing!
Now it springs up; do you not perceive it?
I am making a way in the wilderness
and streams in the wasteland.

Isaiah 43:19

Jesus looked at them and said, "With man this is impossible, but with God all things are possible."

Matthew 19:26

For you created my inmost being;
you knit me together in my mother's womb.
I praise you because I am fearfully and wonderfully made;
your works are wonderful,
I know that full well.

Psalm 139:13–14

Those who look to him are radiant;
their faces are never covered with shame.

Psalm 34:5

For I consider that the sufferings of this present time are not worth comparing with the glory that is to be revealed to us.

Romans 8:18 ESV

However, as it is written:

"What no eye has seen,
what no ear has heard,

and what no human mind has conceived"—
the things God has prepared for those who love him.

1 Corinthians 2:9

My flesh and my heart may fail,
but God is the strength of my heart
and my portion forever.

Psalm 73:26

The name of the LORD is a strong tower;
the righteous man runs into it and is safe.

Proverbs 18:10 ESV

But the hour is coming, and is now here, when the true worshipers will worship the Father in spirit and truth, for the Father is seeking such people to worship him.

John 4:23 ESV

Therefore, since we are receiving a kingdom that cannot be shaken, let us be thankful, and so worship God acceptably with reverence and awe, for our "God is a consuming fire."

Hebrews 12:28-29

Therefore, if anyone is in Christ, he is a new creation. The old has passed away; behold, the new has come.

2 Corinthians 5:17 ESV

I have been crucified with Christ and I no longer live, but Christ lives in me. The life I now live in the body, I live by faith in the Son of God, who loved me and gave himself for me.

Galatians 2:20

So if the Son sets you free, you will be free indeed.

John 8:36

Therefore, there is now no condemnation for those who are in Christ Jesus, because through Christ Jesus the law of the Spirit who gives life has set you free from the law of sin and death.

Romans 8:1–2

So I say, let the Holy Spirit guide your lives. Then you won't be doing what your sinful nature craves.

Galatians 5:16 NLT

But I tell you the truth, it is to your advantage that I go away; for if I do not go away, the Helper (Comforter, Advocate, Intercessor—Counselor, Strengthener, Standby) will not come to you; but if I go, I will send Him (the Holy Spirit) to you [to be in close fellowship with you].

John 16:7 AMP

But the Helper, the Holy Spirit, whom the Father will send in my name, he will teach you all things and bring to your remembrance all that I have said to you.

John 14:26 ESV

Come close to God, and God will come close to you. Wash your hands, you sinners; purify your hearts, for your loyalty is divided between God and the world.

James 4:8 NLT

Let us draw near to God with a sincere heart and with the full assurance that faith brings, having our hearts sprinkled to cleanse us from a guilty conscience and having our bodies washed with pure water.

Hebrews 10:22

But now, O Lord, you are our Father;
we are the clay, and you are our potter;
we are all the work of your hand.

Isaiah 64:8 ESV

For we are God's handiwork, created in Christ Jesus to do good works, which God prepared in advance for us to do.

Ephesians 2:10

Study this Book of Instruction continually. Meditate on it day and night so you will be sure to obey everything written in it. Only then will you prosper and succeed in all you do.

Joshua 1:8 NLT

If you fully obey the Lord your God and carefully follow all his commands I give you today, the Lord your God will set you high above all the nations on earth.

Deuteronomy 28:1

The Lord himself goes before you and will be with you; he will never leave you nor forsake you. Do not be afraid; do not be discouraged.

Deuteronomy 31:8

Trust in the Lord with all your heart
and lean not on your own understanding;
in all your ways submit to him,
and he will make your paths straight.

Proverbs 3:5-6

ABOUT *the* AUTHOR

MADDIE JOY FISCHER is a twenty-five-year-old writer, speaker, and worship leader in St. Louis, Missouri. She is a new wife to Isaiah, the oldest of five siblings, and a born-and-raised pastor's kid. She is also an ambassador (writer) for the LO sister app by Sadie Robertson's ministry, Live Original. Maddie's passion is to point people to Jesus through living a life of surrender. For ten years, she has shared this passion on her social media platforms with a desire to see people grow in knowledge of God's

Word, boldness to proclaim it, and love for the One who it's all about. She continues to take every opportunity she is given to live out the calling God has prepared for her life as He has continued to grow her ministry every step of the way.

CONNECT WITH MADDIE

MaddieeJoy.com

 @MaddieFischer   @Maddiee_Joy